I HATE EVERYONE, EXCEPT YOU

I HATE EVERYONE, EXCEPT YOU

CLINTON KELLY

G

GALLERY BOOKS

NEW YORK   LONDON   TORONTO   SYDNEY   NEW DELHI

Gallery Books
An Imprint of Simon & Schuster, Inc.
1230 Avenue of the Americas
New York, NY 10020

First Gallery Books hardcover edition January 2017

GALLERY BOOKS and colophon are registered trademarks of Simon & Schuster, Inc.

For information about special discounts for bulk purchases, please contact Simon & Schuster Special Sales at 1-866-506-1949 or business@simonandschuster.com.

The Simon & Schuster Speakers Bureau can bring authors to your live event. For more information or to book an event contact the Simon & Schuster Speakers Bureau at 1-866-248-3049 or visit our website at www.simonspeakers.com.

Interior design by Jaime Putorti

Manufactured in the United States of America

10 9 8 7 6 5 4 3 2

Library of Congress Cataloging-in-Publication Data

Names: Kelly, Clinton author.
Title: I hate everyone, except you / Clinton Kelly.
Description: First Gallery Books hardcover edition. | New York : Gallery Books, 2017.
Identifiers: LCCN 2016030621| ISBN 9781476776934 (hardcover) | ISBN 9781476776941 (trade paper)
Subjects: LCSH: Kelly, Clinton. | Television personalities--United States--Biography.
Classification: LCC PN1992.4.K385 A3 2017 | DDC 791.45092 [B]--dc23 LC record available at https://lccn.loc.gov/2016030621

ISBN 978-1-4767-7693-4
ISBN 978-1-4767-7695-8 (ebook)

You, plural, know who you are. I can't imagine clinging to this enormous, minuscule, spinning sphere with anyone else. I thank my lucky stars for you every damn day. No lie.

TABLE OF CONTENTS

I HATE EVERYONE,
EXCEPT YOU

KAMIKAZE

In the spring of 1982, I got it into my head that I needed, more than anything in the whole world, to visit Action Park in New Jersey. The commercials, which played every seven minutes during reruns of *Gilligan's Island* and *The Brady Bunch*, spoke to the deepest desires of my thirteen-year-old soul.

"There's nothing in the world like Action Park," the jingle jangled. Golden-skinned teenagers frolicked in the world's largest wave pool, flashing their symmetrical white teeth. Others shrieked with glee and unconsciously flexed their abs as they whipped through the turns of a water slide. They seemed to be having the best collective puberty ever, free of pimples, braces, and social awkwardness, all of which plagued me more than I cared to admit.

If I could just break into their social circle, I reasoned, my skin would clear up, my teeth would magically align themselves, and I could be the most popular kid at John F. Kennedy Junior High School in Port Jefferson Station, New York. And maybe, just maybe, I would develop even the slightest hint of muscle tone. Currently, when shirtless, I looked less like a boy than a

xylophone, but I would occasionally amuse houseguests by grab-
bing two spoons and playing "Frère Jacques" on my rib cage.

Mike and Terri must have understood the magical powers of
Action Park, because when I asked them at dinner one night to
take me, they actually said yes.

"Awesome," I said. "I need to buy a new bathing suit. I was
thinking something white." (I had recently seen an ad in which
a very tan male model wore white Ocean Pacific short shorts.
He bore a striking resemblance to me—insofar as he too was
bipedal—so obviously we should have identical wardrobes.)

"We'll shop for summer clothes when school is out," Terri
said. That was the usual routine. On the first weekend after the
last day of school, Terri, my mom, would drive my sister Jodi
and me to the mall, buy us whatever we needed to get through
the summer, and then we'd head to the beach. Though it was
never articulated as such, the ritual felt like a reward for surviv-
ing yet another year in the public school system. Just the three
of us, buying new rubber flip-flops and bathing suits. Jumping
waves on Long Island's south shore. Wolfing down hot dogs with
extra sauerkraut from the concessions stand. It was pretty much
the best day of the year, every year. The next such outing would
be our last, however. Terri was pregnant and due in early August.

"Aw, man, I can't wait that long. I wanna go to Action Park
this weekend," I whined.

Spearing a chicken cutlet with his fork, my stepdad, Mike,
said, "It's mid-May. I doubt Action Park is even open."

He was right, of course, which filled me with rage.

Mike was a tough-talking, bearded hairstylist who, much
to my chagrin at the time, had married Terri the previous fall.
He wore black leather jackets. I dreamed of collecting cashmere
sweaters. He rode a Harley-Davidson. I prayed nightly for a

Volvo. He was a quintessential Long Island Italian. I yearned to convert to any form of Protestantism, not because of a firmly held religious ideology, understand, but just so I could officially call myself a "W.A.S.P." He and I had absolutely nothing in common, except for an apparent love of my mother.

The first time I'd met Mike, three years earlier, I had been thoroughly appalled. We were living with my mother's friend Lynn, also recently divorced, and her two kids, Candice and Craig. Another single woman, Heather, and her son, Justin, a year or two older than me, also migrated in and out of the house. Three single women, five kids, three bedrooms. And although everyone knew the arrangement was temporary, it was still pretty weird. And sad. Saturday morning cartoons, for example, are considerably less enjoyable when your mother is asleep under a crocheted afghan on the living room couch.

Mike had stopped by the house one night to pick up Terri for a date. When he arrived, she was still in the bathroom, putting the finishing touches on her hair and makeup. She must have seen him pull into the driveway, because she shouted, "Can one of you let Mike in? Tell him I'll be right out."

Nobody responded. The house was unusually quiet; the other kids were visiting grandparents or dads for the weekend.

"Clint! Did you hear me?"

"Yes," I said and reluctantly got up from the kitchen table, where I had been sitting by myself eating flourescent-orange macaroni and cheese and flipping through the latest issue of *Cosmopolitan*. I opened the door and Mike entered. He wore black leather boots, faded jeans, and a black button-front shirt open about three-quarters of the way down his slim torso. He sported at least three gold chains, dark aviator-style sunglasses, and feathered black hair. Honestly, I would have been less shocked if a 5-foot-10-inch coho salmon had stepped into our foyer.

"You must be Clint," he said. "I'm Mike. Nice to meet you." He extended his hand to shake mine, but I was so flabbergasted by his appearance I could barely lift my arm. My hand just sort of hung there like a limp cabbage leaf. He shook it delicately, as one might have done upon meeting a fancy Victorian lady.

Jodi came running over. She was a cherubic seven-year-old with a perpetually stained face. One day she might have an orange Hi-C smile that extended well past the boundaries of her mouth. The next she could have fallen asleep on a lollypop so that it left a semipermanent green kiss on her cheek. Today she appeared to have been lining her lips with chocolate, at least I *hoped* it was chocolate. I resented her ability to make her Halloween candy last well past Christmas, even into early spring. She ate a half a piece or less of it every day, whereas I ate a pillowcase-worth before November first. A single gobstopper was a weeklong event for Jodi. Sometimes I'd find a half-sucked one hiding in the Connect Four box and roll my eyes. If I was particularly desperate for sugar, I'd rinse it off and eat it myself.

"I'm Jodi!"

"I'm Mike."

"Hi!"

"Hi."

"Bye!"

"Bye." She ran off, back to the TV or her Barbies or the Milky Way she'd been sucking face with.

When it struck me that my mother could possibly marry this dark, hairy man—after all, he was *standing in our foyer*—I decided it was my responsibility to end their budding relation-

ship immediately. Not for any personal reasons. I was just looking out for the best interests of my mother, who at the age of
thirty was obviously experiencing some kind of midlife crisis.
My biological father might not have been perfect—far from it—
but at least he wore a suit to work and *shaved* every day, like a
productive member of society. This degenerate was probably on
welfare.

Mike attempted to make small talk. "So, what grade are
you—"

"My mom's dating a lot of guys," I blurted. "Like, a *lot*."

"Really." He seemed unfazed, but it was hard to get a read
through the aviators.

"Yep," I said. "She told me last night that she doesn't like
any of them."

Still no reaction. "OK," he said.

"So, you're wasting your time with her."

"Am I?"

"For sure. It's just, you know, I don't want to see you get hurt
or anything."

"Gotcha," he said, nodding his head. "I appreciate that."

Like a cool breeze, Terri rounded the corner to where Mike
and I were standing. Most of the time I took her appearance for
granted, but she really was quite beautiful. Tall and slim with
curves in all the conventionally desirable places. Her shoulder-
length black hair was feathered, quite similar to Mike's, actually,
and she had big green eyes that were heavily mascaraed in the
style of the time. Her smile always looked the slightest bit mis-
chievous, even when she was wasn't. Tonight she wore dark jeans,
a white blouse, and a black satin bomber jacket. As she kissed him
hello on the cheek, they struck me as a very exotic couple, perfectly styled to go to a discotheque or knock over a liquor store.

"Sorry to keep you waiting," my mom said. "I see you've met Clint."

"Yeah," said Mike. "We were just having a little chat."

"About what?" she asked, looking at me.

"Stuff," I said.

"What kind of stuff?"

"I was just saying how I got detention this week for running to the school bus," I said.

"Why'd you tell him *that*?" I couldn't tell if Terri was horrified or amused. She explained to Mike that I was having a hard time in this new school district. "That's his second detention this month. He used to be the perfect student, until recently."

"He seems pretty perfect to me," Mike said. If he was being sarcastic, I certainly didn't know it at the time, because I believed I was indeed as perfect as a ten-year-old could be. And why my mother would choose to go out to dinner with this man rather than stay home with me was beyond my comprehension.

Mike and Terri left on their date, and three years later we were a family of four (plus one in utero) living in a much nicer, less-crowded house and eating a lot of chicken cutlets.

Maybe we could go to Action Park some time in July, they said.

"July? I can't wait until July! It probably opens Memorial Day weekend! I need to go then!"

My begging and whining did little to convince them that donning a bathing suit in 60-degree temperatures would be a good idea. We would make the drive to Vernon, New Jersey, in July.

Oh, shit, I thought. *They're coming too.* I hadn't accounted for that possibility. I had figured they would drop me off at the front gate so I could make new and gorgeous friends who loved me for my God-given potential to be cool. But now, Mike and Terri were coming with me and we'd have to walk around a water park together. In bathing suits. With my little sister Jodi in tow. Aw man, my life sucked so much I could barely breathe.

For the next two months I kept Action Park at an emotional distance, the way a kid thinks about Christmas in September or an adult thinks about that STD test they should *probably* get after a long weekend in Miami. The commercials would play every day, and I had no choice but to regard those wet teenagers as long-lost cousins who didn't know I existed but who would embrace me as one of their own upon first sight.

July arrived, eventually, and brought with it a heat wave, as is typical of Long Island summers, and—after some gentle reminding on my part—we loaded into the Chevy Blazer destined for New Jersey. Mike drove, as usual, and didn't seem to mind at all that Jodi and I sang along loudly to Donna Summer's greatest hits album as it played on the built-in 8-track. He wasn't a singer, he said, when we tried to cajole him into joining us.

"Mike! 'Bad Girls' is next!" Jodi yelled. "You can do the *toot toot beep beep* part! It doesn't matter what you sound like! You just say *toot toot awwwww beep beep*!" He smiled and politely declined. She sang it instead, rocking her head back and forth while she did so. She also squinted her eyes and pouted her lips, in what I assumed was a prepubescent attempt at sexiness. I silently wondered if I should care that my ten-year-old sister was really *feeling* this song about street-trolling hookers. I didn't.

Much to my surprise and disappointment, Action Park wasn't brimming with perfect specimens of American adolescence. Most of the people were either kind of fat, or droopy, or hairy. I mean, really disturbingly hairy. Men sprouted hair out of their lower backs and on their shoulders. Hair grew under their arms, across their bellies, up and down their legs into their groins, necks, knuckles, like mold spreading across a shower curtain. The women provided little respite from the assault on my senses. Some had giant, pendulous breasts and thighs the texture of chicken chow mein. Others looked broken or bowlegged, like life had really knocked the crap out of them.

Of course, I had been to the beaches of Long Island countless times, so I knew that human bodies came in all different shapes and sizes. But I had never seen so many half-naked people this close-up. They were practically touching me, making me anxious. I wanted to go home, back to our split-level ranch in the suburbs, where everyone was at least moderately attractive. Where skin clung tautly to our frames. Where hair grew in the *appropriate* places. And where there were no open wounds.

See, Action Park wasn't comprised solely of water rides. It also featured an attraction called the Alpine Slide, a concrete half-pipe-shaped track that meandered down a mountain. People would sit on little nonmotorized sleds, controlling their speed with a joystick. You could pull the stick closer to you to apply the brake or push it forward and let gravity whisk you along the path.

The Alpine Slide had no seat belts or roll bars, just one built-in, state-of-the-art safety system: your epidermis. If you were to fall out of your sled or jump the track, the only structure that might slow your descent down the mountain was your skin.

I'm not exaggerating when I tell you that one-quarter of the people mulling around Action Park did so with a moderate to severe case of road rash, which the first-aid team would cover liberally with Mercurochrome, a bright-red antiseptic that made bloody wounds appear even gorier. One might assume the management of Action Park would forbid, or at the very least discourage, people with fresh cuts and scrapes from entering a communal water ride. Nope. They might as well have posted signs reading, SKINNED HALF YOUR ARM? DON'T BE A PUSSY. JUMP RIGHT BACK IN THE POOL WHERE EVEN MORE OF YOUR BODILY FLUIDS CAN MIX FREELY WITH THOSE OF PERFECT STRANGERS. WE'RE ALL IN THIS TOGETHER!

Another problem with this place was that to ride the Alpine Slide you had to get to the top of the mountain, and the only way to do that was to take a ski lift, which ran above the track itself. Pretty straightforward in its design, sure. Go up ski lift. Go down slide. Now add a few thousand teenage boys to the equation.

See any inherent problem with that?

No?

Well, let me help you out. What do teenage boys like to do from high places?

They spit.

So, as you're zooming down the Alpine Slide, maneuvering around turns, adjusting your speed accordingly using the hand-held brake-joystick, you must also dodge innumerable loogies hocked by New Jersey's future rocket scientists.

When I rode the slide, I was lucky enough to be hit with sputum on the back of my left hand. It could have been much worse, but I was still furious. If anyone was going to goober on me, it should be an attractive person, not some greasy-mulleted punk wearing cutoff jean shorts.

Unsurprisingly, perhaps, the teenage boys tended not to spit on the pretty girls. Instead of mucus, they would hurl compliments, maybe something as subtle as, "Nice tits, blondie!" Or a polite offer to "Sit on my face, bitch!"

On the ride ahead of me was a reasonably attractive red-headed girl of about sixteen. Some boys on the ski lift yelled, "Suck my dick!" and so she flipped them off with both hands. A dumb rookie move. She let go of the brake while taking a turn and flew off the track. There was really no winning when it came to the Alpine Slide, unless you held stock in Mercuro-chrome.

Between the hairy men, the loogie-spitting boys, and the open wounds, this day trip was turning into a disaster, and it was all my fault. Terri was eight months pregnant and waddling around uncomfortably in shorts and a maternity top. Mike wouldn't go on any of the rides because he didn't want to leave my mother alone in her condition. At least that's what he said. That meant I had to supervise Jodi, who wanted to do things that prepubescent girls do, like splash around the shallow end of the wave pool and scream in a pitch that could shatter Austrian crystal.

Usually Mike was a big proponent of "getting our money's worth." That is, arriving at dawn and staying until forcibly removed. But by two in the afternoon everyone was ready to leave Action Park. Even Jodi casually remarked, "Let's go now to avoid rush hour." You know your whole family is having a crappy time when the ten-year-old feigns concern over the traffic patterns on the Long Island Expressway. But it was Saturday, and the rest of us knew that if we left at 2 p.m., traffic would actually be worse because of the beachgoers. Nevertheless, we all jumped right on Jodi's bandwagon.

"Yes!"

"Rush hour!"

"Let's get the hell out of here!"

As we started to leave, though, I was overcome by the feeling that the day was incomplete. I had been deceived by the ad executives who produced the commercials for this place. I had not made any new beautiful, good-natured friends, because there were none to be found. "There's nothing in the world like Action Park," the commercials said. Indeed. There was nothing in the world like this place—if you wanted a staph infection.

I knew what had to be done. I could save this day. By riding Kamikaze.

Kamikaze, suspiciously absent from the TV commercials, was a waterslide conceived by someone with little regard for human life. Shaped like a giant curved L, the slide required its rider to climb a one-hundred-foot tower and, once at the top, enter a cage and cross his arms. The ride operator would then press a button, releasing the floor of the cage and dropping the rider into a free fall. Because the slide is completely vertical at first, the rider's body does not touch the slide until it bends to 90 degrees and enters a series of shallow hills and approximately six inches of water.

"I'm going to ride that," I said.

"What?" said Terri. She wasn't incredulous; she couldn't hear me because I was whispering. The words had slipped out of my mouth before I could suck them back in. Even with what little life experience I had, I knew Kamikaze was designed for grown men with diminished mental capacity, sort of an experiment in natural selection.

"He said he wants to ride that!" Jodi yapped.

"Absolutely not," Terri said. "You'll kill yourself. Let's go home. Remember, it's rush hour."

"C'mon, Ter," Mike said. "Let him ride it if he wants." Great. Now Mike was involved. I really couldn't tell if he was defending my budding manhood or if he finally saw his opportunity to destroy me and get my mother to himself.

Mom asked, "Do you really think it's safe?"

"Take a look," he answered. "Nobody's been carried off on a stretcher yet."

It was true. Grown men were indeed walking away after riding Kamikaze, but most of them stumbled as though they were recovering from a frying pan to the frontal cortex.

"OK. Just be careful," Terri said.

"Yes," Mike said, "be careful." He was smiling the same smile he had when dropping Jodi and me off at our grandparents' house for the weekend, except this time it was bigger, like he expected me to be gone for more than two days.

I started off to the steps of Kamikaze and heard Jodi call after me: "Don't die!" Sweet kid.

I climbed the metal stairs, occasionally pausing to see if my family was looking. They were. I could see my mother holding her round belly with one hand and shielding her eyes from the sun with the other. Jodi was holding Mike's hand.

Because so few people wanted to ride Kamikaze, there was no wait when I reached the top. A kid barely older than me told me to step into the cage and cross my arms. His name tag read KEVIN. "You'll probably want to keep your legs together," Kevin said without looking at me. He was reading a magazine about dirt bikes.

Keep my legs together? Why the hell was I doing this? To prove something to myself? To Mike? To my mother? My heart was pounding through my emaciated chest. I wondered if Kevin could see it vibrating like a berserk squirrel trapped behind my sternum. I could die right now or become paralyzed, I knew, and yet to climb back down those steps, with half of New Jersey watching, would have been more humiliating than to live the rest of my life with a torn spinal cord and the mental capacity of a parsnip.

I glanced at Kevin, who had raised his head from his magazine to make sure I was standing as instructed. I wondered what
kind of family Kevin came from, whether his parents were proud
that he had a job at Action Park. He looked a little dead in the
eyes, so I concluded that he came from a home in which his
father drank too much beer and his mother smoked cigarettes at
the kitchen table while wearing a floral housecoat. Would Kevin
cry if I died? Or would he brag to his dirt-bike-loving friends
that he helped kill a skinny kid who was probably a fag? Most
likely the latter.

Kevin pressed a button and the floor dropped from beneath
me, sending the Human Xylophone plummeting to earth, clad
in nothing but a white bathing suit at least two sizes too big.
(Terri and I hadn't been able to find the coveted white trunks
in the boys' department, so I convinced her to buy me a men's
small. *Look, Mom, I can tie the drawstring really tight! They're not
too big!* To give you a little perspective: My waist at the time was
about 26 inches. A men's small is 30. Those extra four inches will
prove important in just a minute.)

I free-fell for less than a second before my body made contact with the slide, which came as sweet relief, and before I knew
it I had begun the turn from vertical to horizontal. I cascaded
over a few small humps and continued down the chute to where
the deeper water slowed me to a complete stop.

Unfortunately, that deeper water, combined with my high
speed of travel, spread my spindly legs apart and jerked my too-
big bathing suit severely to the right and halfway up my torso.
Upon realizing that my barely teenage privates were now on dis-
play for a small but significant fraction of New Jersey to see, I
yanked the suit back down to cover myself before anyone could
notice.

I stood up, a little shaky but in one piece. Stumbling back to my family, I was greeted like a soldier returning from war. Or a dog that ran away for a couple of hours.

"That was crazy," Mike said with a laugh. "I'm really impressed."

Terri added, "You were definitely the youngest guy to go on that thing."

"I'm glad you're not dead," Jodi said.

I mumbled some thanks to the three of them and assumed the funny feeling in my pelvis was because I had just cheated death.

"OK, let's hit the road," Mike said. "Does anyone need to use the bathroom? It's a long ride home."

Jodi said she didn't, which was unusual because she had a strange affinity for public restrooms. Clearly, she had peed in the wave pool until her bladder was empty.

"I guess I'll go," I said.

The men's room at Action Park was one of those places where you never want to find yourself. I mean, if some sort of sadistic genie ever forces you to choose between spending time in a Ugandan prison or a similar amount of time in the Action Park men's room during a heat wave, choose the men's room. Otherwise, avoid it at all cost. There are just too many wet, hairy guys in drippy suits and bare feet mingling with all the smells of humanity.

Back in 1982, there weren't dividers between urinals. If you had to pee, you would do it shoulder-to-shoulder with a stranger, in this case a shirtless stranger. I chose the far-right urinal, so there was a wall to my right and a man to my left. Men's room etiquette dictates that you don't look too closely at other men, but I could tell he was a big-boned, New Jersey dad type.

So, I get ready to pee, but before anything comes out, I realize I have to . . . well . . . fart. So, I fart.

Except this fart doesn't make the usual *pfft* sound. It makes a splash on the concrete floor.

I stood frozen in pure terror. Holding my penis, looking straight ahead at the wall, I could see with my peripheral vision that the man next to me has glanced down at the floor and now he was staring at me. I turned my head slowly to the left and upward to meet his gaze.

We were two strangers looking into each other's eyes in a hot, wet men's room. This man, with the bulbous nose and a smattering of acne scars across his cheeks, has the power to make this the worst day of my life or to provide a glimmer of sympathy. I steeled myself for a laugh or a snide remark, but mostly I was hoping for a kind word or two. *Say it, buddy. Whatever you're going to say, say it now.*

Without the slightest change in his facial expression—not even a raised eyebrow—he turned to face forward and continued his pee. He said nothing. Nothing.

I looked down to the small, thankfully clear, puddle between my feet. I felt like something needed to be said, if only to prove this was actually happening. To prove that I am in this men's room right now, that I haven't died on the waterslide and my soul isn't floating aimlessly from urinal to urinal in search of The Light.

"Kamikaze," I whispered.

Still expressionless, he shook his penis, flushed, and left. I would never see him again.

The ride back to Long Island was pretty quiet. None of us was in the mood for Kenny Rogers or Donna Summer. At some point, around Nassau County, Jodi fell asleep in the car.

"Something tells me that wasn't the day you were expecting," Mike said.

"Nah, not really."

"You're being really quiet. Is everything OK?" he asked.

"I guess."

My mother knew I was lying. "What's wrong?"

"Water came out of my butt," I said.

Mike and Terri looked at each other, startled.

Terri craned her neck around to look at me in the backseat. "Did it come out of your butt right now?" she asked.

"No!" I barked. "In the bathroom. At Action Park."

"In the toilet?"

"Standing up."

Mike looked at me through the rearview mirror. I could tell he was wide-eyed, even through his dark aviators. "Was it just . . . water?" he asked.

"Yes, it was just water! Oh my God, I knew I shouldn't have told you! Can we please not talk about this anymore? I wish I was *dead*."

"Aw, don't say that," Terri said, then I wished I hadn't.

"So, you got a little water up your ass. There are worse things in the world," Mike offered. "You rode Kamikaze, man! You couldn't *pay* me to do that." He was smiling, which made my eyes well up, because my embarrassment was giving way to the realization that Mike was proud of me on some level, and that we were becoming a little family, with another member on the way.

BRILLIANT IDEAS

Jennifer's new sofa had been delivered that morning, so she invited me to her apartment to see it, and presumably to sit on it.

A purchase of furniture neither disposable nor secondhand was company-worthy at this point in our lives. We were in our late twenties, living paycheck-to-paycheck, the vast majority of those paychecks going toward the rent for our Upper East Side apartments. I lived in a small rent-stabilized one-bedroom, located precisely a mop's-length away from the uptown exit ramp of the Fifty-Ninth Street Bridge. Because the car exhaust would regularly cover the living room's two windows with a semiopaque layer of grime, once a week I would stand on my fire escape and clean them with a sponge-head mop I had purchased specifically for this task.

Most drivers inching along in the ceaseless traffic of the exit ramp would pretend not to see me standing outside in my boxer shorts and an oversized T-shirt, leaning over the second-floor railing, mop outstretched and a plastic bucket overflowing with suds at my side. But I could sense their vague suspicion. *Is he trying to make money by mopping stopped cars? Don't make eye contact. Don't make eye contact. Keep your mop off my Toyota Corolla.*

Occasionally, on a really hot morning, a driver with all his windows down, most likely because his car's AC wasn't functioning, would attempt to strike up a conversation with me.

"Hot out, huh."

"Yup," I'd reply.

"Dirty windows, huh?"

"Yup."

"That's what you get for living next to a bridge."

"Wait. This is a bridge? I thought you were all waiting in line to go to hell."

"Eh, fuck you."

I'd shake the mop in his direction as if to say, *Don't make me use this thing on you, because I will.*

Once, a woman in the passenger seat of a minivan rolled down her window to ask me where York Avenue was. I pointed east with the mop, dripping some soapy gray liquid on myself in the process. "I told you so, Hal," she barked at her husband. "I'm sorry," she said to me, "my husband is an idiot. I hope one day you get a better apartment."

Jennifer's apartment was a bit more posh than mine; it was a sublet in the high-rise famous for its cameo in the opening credits of *The Jeffersons*. Every time I entered the lobby, I imagined myself as the meat in a George-and-Weezy sandwich, him proudly strutting on my left and her on my right, regarding it all in wide-eyed wonderment. I'd press the elevator button and fantasize about the dinner Florence would have waiting for us, maybe meat loaf with a side of sass. And perhaps tonight would be the night Mr. Bentley would let me walk on his back.

The first few times I visited Jennifer, I'd sing *The Jeffersons'* theme at her apartment door: "Now we're up in the big leagues, gettin' our turn at bat!"

She'd inevitably shush me in her politely paranoid way; she didn't want to bother the neighbors, lest they rat her out for her not being on the lease.

Jennifer had quickly become my best friend in New York. We met a few years earlier while we were both working as home-shopping hosts for Q2, a short-lived offshoot of QVC that broadcast live from Silvercup Studios in Queens. She was gorgeous, and I hated her on sight. When an executive for the company introduced us, Jennifer gave me a weak smile and kept her arms folded across her chest. *She thinks she's better than me*, I told myself. *I'm going to make her life miserable.*

The next day she apologized for the lukewarm reception. She explained that she was hungover, the air-conditioning was too high, and she was wearing a thin bra. "Boing!" She pointed her index fingers away from her boobs. I knew we'd be friends forever.

Her sofa was nice, I supposed, a seafoam-green convertible, smallish but the right size for her alcove studio. I had helped her pick it out, mildly jealous the whole time we shopped because she could afford one while I was still sleeping on a futon. She was making more money as a commercial actress than I was as a freelance writer and editor. I had given commercial acting a shot but quit after my first audition, which Jennifer's agent—at her prodding—had set up for me. It was for Boar's Head Turkey.

The casting director, a blasé gay-ish guy maybe a decade my senior, pointed a video camera in my direction and took a seat behind an industrial folding table. "You're a radio announcer," he said, "and your line is, 'Boar's Head Turkey.'"

"So you want me to say 'Boar's Head Turkey' as though I'm a radio announcer."

"That's what I just said, except in reverse."

"Gotcha." I cupped a hand to my ear (the way radio announcers do?) and produced my most resonant tone: "Boarrrrr's Head Turkey."

"OK, do it again."

A little more gusto this time. "Booooarrrrrrr's Head Turkey!"

"Again."

Maybe I wasn't accentuating the right syllable. "Booooar's Head TUR-key!"

"Again."

"BoaRRRRR's Head Tur-KEY."

"Again."

"BOOOOOARS Head Turrrrr-key."

"Again."

"Boarrr's HEAD Tur-KEYYYY."

"Again."

I was stuck in a sadistic loop with this fucker. He knew I'd never get the part, but he was making me repeat this damn line over and over. I couldn't think of any new ways to say it! I was barely intelligible at this point. It was like that scene at the end of *The Miracle Worker* when Anne Bancroft gets Patty Duke to say "water" but it sounds like "wwwaaaaaauuhh-waaaahhhhwuh."

I refused to be the first to quit.

"BWOOORRRS HEHD TUH-TUH."

"Again."

"TURRRRRRRR GA-BWAW BWAH."

"Again."

"BUHHHH HUH TURRRR TURRRR."

"Again."

A knock at the door. His assistant, asking if he was ready for the next auditioner.

"Yes, send him in. Thank you Mister . . . Kelly."

"You are . . . welcome."

I waited years for that commercial to make its way to television, just so I could see who beat me out for the role of self-loathing, turkey-loving radio announcer, but it never aired. While Jennifer opened a bottle of wine and assembled a cheese platter in the kitchen, I perused the magazines on her coffee table. I had already read that week's *People* and *Entertainment Weekly*, so I flipped through another I had never heard of: *Marie Claire*.

Opening to a feature story titled "How Many Men Have You Slept with This Week?," I was instantly sucked in, so to speak. But I was even more intrigued by the women holding up signs with big, bold numbers like "3" and "0" and "1" and "27." By the time Jennifer came back to her new sofa, I had gobbled up every word of the article.

"What is this magazine?" I asked.

"*Marie Claire*. I like it."

"It is literally the most ridiculous thing I have ever seen. I need to work there."

"Uh. OK," she said.

"Do you mind if I rip out the masthead?"

"Take the whole thing if you want."

"That's OK. I don't want to be seen carrying this rag around." I tore the masthead containing all the editors' names and the address of the Hearst offices, folded it, and put it into my pocket.

We drank wine and talked about men and our careers and the television shows we should write, like the one about the gay guy and the straight girl who are best friends living in New York City who have some wacky neighbors and go on crazy dates. "There's nothing like it on TV!" When *Will & Grace* premiered the next year, Jennifer was convinced NBC had bugged her apartment.

When I returned home, I drafted a letter to the editor-in-chief, Glenda Bailey. Glenda. Glenda. The name floated through my mind like an incantation. Glennnndah. Glennnndah. I had never met a Glenda before, though I had driven through Glendale once on the way to Disneyland. How exotic Glenda seemed. She would be the woman to change my life, I decided, and so I mentally grouped her with other G names that positively influenced me, like Glinda the Good Witch of the North and Glen the First Guy I Ever Made Out With.

Dear Ms. Bailey,

I don't know you and you don't know me. I don't even know anyone who knows you, but I want to be an editor at Marie Claire.

I'd like to meet with you, and to make it worth your while I will come to our meeting with 100 original story ideas for your magazine.

My résumé is attached.

Thank you for your time,

Clinton Kelly

Two weeks after mailing it, I received a call.

"Can I speak to Ms. Kelly?" asked the woman on the other end of the line.

"This is Mr. Kelly."

"Oh, you're a man."

"Mostly."

"Glenda Bailey of *Marie Claire* asked me to call you. She'd like you to come in for a meeting tomorrow."

"Tomorrow?" I asked. I had been planning on doing my laundry.

"Yes. Can you do first thing in the morning? She's quite busy."

"Sure. What time is first thing?"

"Eight thirty."

"OK. I'll be there."

I hung up the phone and walked three blocks to Blooming-dale's to buy something to wear. I couldn't meet Glenda in Banana Republic khakis and a polo shirt. A meeting with Glennnndah required something dressier, perhaps an Elizabethan neck ruff. But I settled on a black suit and lavender shirt, which together cost $800, a virtual drop in the bucket compared to my $45,000 credit-card and student-loan debt.

On the way home reality hit me: I had to come up with one hundred story ideas by the morning. A couple of headlines had been floating around my brain in the two weeks I had been waiting for a response: "What Makes Me Different Makes Me Beautiful," an article showcasing women who had features they might have hated at one point in their lives but learned to love, like unruly hair, lots of freckles, or a gap-toothed smile; "48-Hour Closet Swap," for which two women with polar-opposite styles would trade wardrobes for two days and report how differently strangers, mostly men, treated them.

I've never been especially good at math, but even I knew that two stories out of one hundred made me exactly 2 percent ready for the next day's first-thing meeting. Crap. I bought two bottles of Sancerre, which I also could not afford, and invited Jennifer over for a brainstorming session. Luckily, she was free.

By the time Jen arrived, another bottle of Sancerre in hand, I had about fifty semisolid ideas. And over the next few hours we came up with another twenty-five—mostly stories about dating and sex—until we hit a point of diminishing returns. Neither of us had eaten dinner, and we were getting pretty drunk.

"You know what I'd like to read?" Jennifer asked. "A story about a chubby girl with a mole on her chin who had the mole removed and lost the weight and grew up to be a beautiful commercial actress and television host."

"That's amazing," I replied. "But do you know anyone I could interview for that?"

"Hey! That's my story!"

"Oh, right. I had forgotten you had that mole," I lied. "I'll write the headline down and see if they go for it. How do you feel about: 'How My Mole Made Me Whole'?"

"That sounds like there's a mole near my hole," she said.

"Not if you read it. See?" I showed her the computer monitor. "It's whole. Spelled with a w."

"I still don't like it."

"How about 'Wholly Moley'?" I asked.

"Forget about the mole," she said. "The mole is irrelevant."

"So what you're telling me is . . . this is a story about moles and the women who love them."

"That is not even close to what I am telling you."

"Jennifer, you are an ideas machine," I said. "I am going to propose a series of first-person stories about women who have used their skin conditions to their romantic advantage. 'He Loves Me Warts and All, Like Literally.'"

"That's disgusting."

"'Rash Decisions: A Seven-Year Itch Worth Scratching.'"

"Gross."

"'Psoriasis Shmoriasis: Our Love Isn't the Only Thing Inflamed.' These ideas write themselves!"

"I'm going home." And she did.

I woke up the next morning with a mild hangover and a level of career excitement I hadn't felt in years, if at all. *This is my big break*, I told myself, *my dream of being a real live magazine editor is about to come true.* I'll work in a fancy office surrounded by glamorous people. I'll be paid six figures just to attend meetings and spout ideas off the top of my head like "21 G-Spots You Never Knew You Had!" and "Celebrities with Weird Thumbs!" and "Put 'Er There: Sex on Top of Unexpected Furniture!" I'll have health insurance and a gym membership and receive tons of attention at parties—just for showing up. I'll be slightly aloof but amused by the social climbers, men and women alike, trying to get into my pants. Maybe I'll make out with one or two of them, then laugh when they ask to come home with me. Ha! Not just anyone is getting a slice of this meat. I'm saving it for other high-powered creative types who can appreciate my ruthless ambition and general *je ne sais quoi*. And I'll buy some curtains, so commuters from Queens can't get so much as a glimpse into my morning routine of drinking coffee and embellishing the mildly flirtatious banter between Katie Couric and Matt Lauer. "Oh, you tell him, Katie! Girl, your legs have been polished to a high sheen this morning!" You know what? Fuck the curtains and fuck this whole apartment! I'll leave this dump tomorrow with all the Ikea furniture in it. And you can keep the security deposit too, Mister Landlord Who Never Understood Me Anyhow, with all your wanting-the-rent-on-time bullshit. Don't you know who I am now? I'm Clinton Kelly, the most fabulous man in the world!

I dashed off the last twenty-five or so story ideas, stupid women's magazine weight-loss stories like "Lose 10 Pounds by Yesterday," and put on my new suit, which I discovered had a small hole in the crotch. I vowed to keep my legs together.

The lobby of the *Marie Claire* editorial department was just slightly more glamorous than that of a medical-supply firm in Akron. Glenda's assistant stuck her head out the door. "I'm sorry, but Glenda can't see you today," she said. "She's preparing for some press surrounding the upcoming issue." The assistant said I could meet with Michele, the deputy editor, when she arrived, probably some time before ten. I could come back later or wait.

"I'll hang out here in the lobby," I said. *Yep, I'll just sit in that plastic chair facing the door, watching my dreams rot like a bowl of fruit on time-lapse video. Thanks so much.*

Employees began to arrive, coffees in hand, and quite frankly, I had expected them to be better looking. I had imagined lots of people, mostly women, who were almost exquisite enough to be models, but not quite, so they would have to be content working in the next-best industry, fashion magazine publishing. I pictured perfect-featured girls who were a mere five foot seven. "Too short, sorry. It'll be a life of magazines for you." And others who were stunning but asymmetrical. "Dear, your left eye is one millimeter larger than your right. I'm afraid you can never model. But would you care to be an accessories editor?"

Overall, they were just slightly better-than-average looking. Sure, some of them were so skinny you could see through them, but they didn't look happy about it. I had been expecting to work among anorexic women who radiated inner strength, not soul-crushing hunger. And what was with all the joyless denim? The office was like a GAP ad in Kazakhstan.

Michele arrived: gray trousers, an untucked sleeveless peach button-front blouse, not a single accessory. Her shoulder-length brown hair was unbrushed and damp. She also wore no discernable makeup, so I wasn't surprised when she spoke to me in an English accent. All of the British women I had ever met in New York City had that drip-dried kind of look.

"Glenda's assistant says you have an appointment. Come with me, I suppose," she said with formal politeness. She had a strong and swift stride as she led me through the office. "That's Glenda over there," she said, tilting her head to the left toward a glass-walled corner office, where a handsome woman sat at her desk scowling at her computer, oblivious to the two stylists violently tugging and drying her hair.

So that's the mythical Glennnndah. And she's blowing me off for a blowout. I wonder if the subscribers know about this, I thought. *That when they spend their hard-earned money on a copy of* Marie Claire *it's going directly into Glenda Bailey's scalp.* This was outrageous. When I got home I would write an exposé of some kind to be published by some kind of feminist newsletter. I would need to do some research on that. But in all honesty, I was so jealous I could spit. I wanted that corner office so bad and I wanted a blowout by someone other than Beth at Supercuts with the lazy eye who for the life of her just could not figure out how to tame my multiple cowlicks.

Michele's office was also glassed-in, with none of the sophistication of Glenda's. Magazines and newspapers were strewn everywhere, with large piles of manuscripts and manila folders on her desk.

"Why are you here exactly?" Michele asked.

"I wrote Glenda a letter. I believe it's in that envelope you're holding. I said that if she would just meet with me, I'd give her one hundred story ideas."

When she removed the cover letter and résumé, I could see that someone, probably Glenda, had written "CALL HER" at the top.

"You're not a woman," Michele said.

"People around here seem surprised by that. It's starting to give me a complex. I mean I know I'm a little effeminate, but . . ."

"Just a little." She smiled. "So, where are these story ideas?"

I had been carrying them around, not in a briefcase, but in a brand new manila folder, which was starting to look a little worse for wear. "Right here." I passed them across her desk, feeling like a failure because the tab where I had written "*Marie Claire*" had become a little bent during my ride on the crosstown bus.

Michele picked up a ballpoint pen and read the list, making little check marks next to some ideas and slash marks through others, while I watched.

"Brilliant. Brilliant," she mumbled, not lifting her eyes from the pages. "Did it. Not us. Not us . . ." She continued for a few minutes until she paused to make eye contact with me. "'How My Mole Made Me Whole'? What is that about?"

Oh, the terror. I had neglected to delete that one!

"Well, ummmm, I was thinking we could do a story on people who had moles and other skin conditions."

"Really?" Michele asked.

"No. That one was a joke."

She returned to the list. "Brilliant. Brilliant. Not us. Did it. Not us . . ." And after ten minutes, she counted the number of check marks. "Twenty-three," she said.

Twenty-three was not a hundred. Was I being graded on a curve or on a straight percentage? "Is that good?" I asked.

"It's twenty-three more ideas than I had when I walked in the door," Michele said. I liked her. She was no-bullshit, but nice about it. "Are you looking for writing work?"

"Actually, I want a job as an editor."

"I'll keep you in mind," she said. "Can you find your way out?"

I said I could.

The hairstylists were now putting the finishing touches on Glenda's mane, which had been formed into a soft helmet surrounding her face. I walked past in my black suit and lavender shirt open at the collar. Take a look at what you missed out on,

Glennnndah Bailey, Dasher of Dreams, in your fancy corner office. Look at me, I willed her. *Look at me!*

She didn't.

I ended up being offered a job at *Marie Claire* as a contributing editor for a lot less money than I had hoped, but I accepted it anyway. Professionally, it may have been the most miserable year of my life. I shared a tiny office with three women, all of whom were very lovely, but we had zero privacy or personal space. I heard every word of their telephone conversations, and they every word of mine, work-related or not. We knew too much about one another: who had a doctor's appointment, who had a date, who was fighting with their mother. I would drink gallons of water a day, just to have an excuse to leave my desk and pee in the usually empty men's room.

By default I became the "What Do Men Think of Your _____?" editor, and so I'd have to produce a seemingly endless stream of stories filling in that blank. What do men think of your hair? Of your shoes? Of your bedroom? Of your complete inability to think for yourself?

Sometimes they ran in the magazine, sometimes not. That was the job: have twenty or so stories cooking on the back burner at any given time so that Glenda could pull one out randomly and tell you (via Michele) it was going to press tomorrow and demand to know why it wasn't completely ready to go to press today.

I did end up producing "What Makes Me Different Makes Me Beautiful." It took six months to convince Glenda (via Michele) that the story was a good idea. I found women willing to discuss the physical features they learned to embrace over time. While I was happy with the text, the finished spread didn't come out exactly as I had hoped, thanks to the photo department. They ran a dramatic profile shot of the girl with supercurly hair, who also had a considerable nose, showcasing the fact that she had *two* prominent characteristics, not just *one*. The art was slightly confusing, but the editorial was crystal-clear. Nevertheless, Glenda held it up during the joyless monthly staff meeting. She said, in her nasal English accent, "I don't *understannnnd*. Is this story about her *hair* or her *nose*?"

"It's about her hair," I said. "I'm not sure why art chose that particular image, because it does make her nose look huge, but in the piece she talks only about her hair."

"Did you know she had a big nose when you cast her for the story?" Glenda asked.

"I had seen a photo of her. It didn't look particularly large from the front."

"Well, I think the story was a bit unsuccessful," she said, and flipped to the next article.

I knew then I had to find a new job. I had assumed that working at a woman's magazine would be more fun, that the real, live women working there would understand how trivial most of the topics we covered—celebrities, hair, sex, shoes, celebrities with hair having sex with shoes—were in the grand scheme of the Universe. But they didn't. They took every aspect of the job incredibly seriously, as they should have. The women I worked with were smart. Really smart. I thought the overall vibe would be a little more "Wink-wink, nudge-nudge. We're all just here to pay our rent, so let's write silly stories about orgasms and lipstick." But they were too professional for that.

I learned what I always knew, that entertainment is a big business, the end goal of which is to make money. And when money's involved, people can be less fun than you'd hope.

On the bus that evening, on my way home from work, I sat a row behind and across from a woman who was flipping through the newest issue of *Marie Claire*. She was in her midtwenties, black, with natural hair held back from her face with a headband. She opened "What Makes Me Different Makes Me Beautiful," and stopped. Watching her read every word of that piece, I wanted so much to tap her on the shoulder and say, "I produced that! The story you're reading—that was my idea!" But I didn't. When she finished that article, she moved on to the next. I'll never know if it so much as crossed her mind ever again.

Jennifer stopped by my apartment in Tribeca on a recent spring evening to see my new wallpaper: black-and-white flowers the size of dinner plates that serve as a background for huge Technicolor butterflies.

"It looks like something in a magazine," she said. "A very, very *gay* magazine."

"That's the look I was going for, something ripped from the pages of *Fancy Fag*, the magazine for the highfalutin homo."

"I love it."

"Thanks. Me too."

Jen lives in a beautiful, tasteful apartment on the Upper West Side now. She's still beautiful and charming as ever. Sometimes, when our husbands are out of town, we'll get together and gab about the old days. We'll also get together with our husbands, but they've both heard the stories of our twenties too many times to find them the slightest bit interesting. They never ask us to stop the reminiscing, however. Their eyes just glaze over politely.

I opened a bottle of Sancerre from the refrigerator and poured us two glasses.

Jen had taken a seat in the hot-pink round swivel chair. One foot was tucked under her, the other was rocking her back and forth. "Can you believe it's nine o'clock and I'm already tired? Remember how we would stay up until three a.m., coming up with ideas for TV shows?"

"I do," I said, handing her a glass. "The only time I see three a.m. now is when I have to get up to pee for the second time. How ridiculous it all seems now."

"What do you mean?" she asked. "Ridiculous how?"

"I don't know," I said.

"I don't think it was ridiculous at all." She was very earnest all of a sudden. "We were being creative. We were having fun. Do you really think we were ridiculous?"

I didn't know how to answer her question. When I look back at my late twenties, my life does seem a little ridiculous. All the time I spent worrying about which designer sweater to wear, who to sleep with because they were more attractive than me, who not to sleep with because they weren't, which bar to be seen in, which bar was dead, which music to listen to. It seems like a huge waste of mental energy. I could have been doing something *important*, I tell myself, sometimes. But what difference does it make? The past is . . . dead. Most of those bars no longer exist, the men I slept with are old and gray, the sweaters I wore lie decomposing in a landfill. I am here now, happily in my present, with a foot in the future.

"We weren't ridiculous at all," I said.

"Good," Jen said. "I didn't think so. Do you mind putting on the AC? It's a little hot in here."

"I'll open a window," I said and got up from my spot on the sofa. As I lifted the sash I noticed that a recent rainstorm had left streaks on the outside of the glass. I made a mental note to have them cleaned the next day.

AUDITIONS, THE UNIVERSE, AND OTHER WHATNOT

My dearest Fanny,

I've been meaning to write you this letter for quite some time. I apologize for the delay, but in my own defense, I didn't know how to get in touch with you. It's difficult to determine the address of a person whose name is an utter mystery! I hope you don't mind I've decided to call you Fanny, as you were such a fan of *What Not to Wear*. The play on words amuses me, but perhaps even more enjoyable are the memories it evokes of Fannie Flagg flaunting her immeasurable wit and charm on *Match Game*.

I won't assume you are a fan of mine, mostly because I can't bear the thought of having "fans." Seems a tad adolescent, *n'est-ce pas*? But I do feel comfortable calling you a fan of the show and what it represented. If you happen to like me as a person, or what you may know of me as a television personality, I consider myself honored. I hope that one day we can meet in person so I can look you in the eyes and tell you that I appreciate all you've done for me. I will not call you Fanny at that point in time—unless Fanny is your actual name. Wouldn't that be something special.

So, about *What Not To Wear*, the show that changed the course of my life and the lives of so many others. My feelings are so . . . complicated, I barely know where to begin, and so I will begin before the beginning. Do you believe in Destiny, Fanny? I'm not sure I do, to be honest. She seems like a concept used to explain the acquisition of power by powerful people. "It was his *destiny* to become the King." And what about Fate? How do you feel about her? Is Fate just the sad sister of Destiny? "It was his *fate* to die alone and penniless." It seems to me like bad luck and poor choices determine one's fate, whereas good luck and deliberate choices result in one's destiny.

Am I getting too heady for you, my dear? I apologize. I am nothing more than an armchair philosopher and not a particularly dedicated one at that. At least not anymore. I spent ten years in psychotherapy—just once a week, nothing too serious—mostly talking through the contradictions and inconsistencies of organized religion. I bet you didn't know that about me, did you? And you know, the older I get (I'm an ancient forty-seven as I write to you today), the less Destiny and Fate—and their cousin Faith, for that matter—concern me. For some, the opposite is true. Men and women on their deathbeds, old as the Appalachians, wondering what it was "all about." So foolish. I must admit, perhaps to the detriment of your esteem for me, that my sympathy for such wonderers is minimal. Imagine being given a life and not understanding until its ugly end that the point was to live it.

So I do not believe it was Fate or Destiny, yet on some level I do believe it was "meant to be." Allow me to tell you the story of how I was cast on the show, and you can decide for yourself whether it was a cocreative act, the Universe being my cocreator, or just a coincidence.

My friend Nancy had been visiting me in New York City. (Her name is Alaya now, but she was certainly Nancy then.) We were (and still are) friends from our undergraduate days at Boston College, despite the fact that the first time I met her I loathed her, but only by association. She looked like a young Jessica Lange, which I found intimidating, and she was dating my freshman-year roommate, whom I hated, and he hated me, if you can believe that! I'm not sure there was any solid reason for all of this hatred; just a visceral reaction among eighteen-year-olds from different corners of the country. So ridiculous! When Alaya and I discuss it now, as we sometimes do, we wonder whether we were all locked in some sort of vicious love triangle in a past life.

I don't know whether I believe in past lives, but they are fun to imagine, aren't they? I've done two past-life regressions, if you can believe it. In one, I was a Philadelphian businessman in the early 1900s! I had a wife, two daughters, and a big belly. I must have been doing well financially, because we lived in a lovely brownstone with elaborate moldings and ceiling medallions. In the other, I was a goat farmer somewhere in the mountains. Could it have been Nepal? Bhutan? Somewhere around there. The location doesn't matter because I don't think I, the goat farmer, could have picked out the town on a map. I was just a quiet little man with sun-darkened and -hardened skin whose goats were taken by an invading army. That's the part at which I snapped myself out of the regression. Too sad to experience (again?).

Where was I? Oh, yes, Nancy was at my apartment for a visit from San Francisco. Or maybe she was living in Seattle at that time. I don't remember, but I do recall she had recently completed a course to "awaken" her "light body." While I don't

understand *exactly* what that entails, I gather it's about expand-
ing one's spiritual consciousness. I've thought about awakening
my own light body, but my gut tells me to leave it sound asleep.
Nobody enjoys being roused from a good, solid nap. I can guarantee you my light body would be really crabby.

I confessed to Nancy that I felt as though I was meant to be
doing something different with my career—I was working as a
magazine editor—but I couldn't put my finger on what it was. She
suggested I ask the Universe for guidance. I wasn't quite sure how to
do that until I read a couple of books by Caroline Myss, in which
she explained that if you ask the Universe for help, it will provide
help. But the catch, she said, is you must put your complete trust in
the Universe. Otherwise, you're just asking the Universe to give you
what you want, not what the Universe knows you need.

Are you still with me, Fanny? This might be too wingding
for you. Or it might offend your religious beliefs. If so, I'm sorry
to have lost you, but I'm just telling a story.

So one night before bed, I performed some deep-breathing
exercises, calming my thoughts so that I could focus on having
a conversation with the Universe, and I said these exact words
aloud: "Universe, I don't know what I'm supposed to be doing
with my life, but if you point me in the right direction, I promise
to follow, no questions asked." And that was it. I went to sleep.

Two weeks later, I received an e-mail from a casting agent
named Barbara Barna asking me if I would like to audition for
a show called *What Not to Wear*. The producers were recasting
the male lead and looking for a replacement with some fashion
experience. I returned her e-mail, attaching a recent photo and
résumé, and we set up an audition for the next day.

When I agreed to the audition, I never thought I'd get the
job. I showed up for that first audition, and Barbara pointed a

video camera at me and asked me to state my name. Then on a nearby television she played a VHS tape of women walking down the streets of Manhattan and asked me to provide color commentary on their outfits. You can probably imagine the critiques I gave. "Suntan hose! How come nobody told me it was 1972 in Boca Raton?" "Your mom called, she wants her jeans back. And she's not sure who your father is." "Honey, that much titty is completely inappropriate—unless you're stripping or having a mammogram."

I left the audition thinking there was no way in hell anyone could have found value in that claptrap, but by the time I got back to my desk, I had received a voice mail asking if I was available for a callback two days later. Evidently, I was just the sort of moderately snarky homosexual they were looking for.

When I arrived at that first callback, there were several men in the reception area outside the studio awaiting their turn to enter. The TV was playing episodes of *What Not to Wear*, which I had still not seen. (There was no video on demand back in those days, Fanny. We were savages.) So I sat and watched the show.

And I hated it.

Good Lord, was it awful! I thought, *If this is the kind of program they want to make, I am the absolute wrong person for it.* The way Stacy and Wayne, the guy they were replacing, spoke to the women on the show felt so mean-spirited and judgmental. Sure, at the time I got a kick out of criticizing people's clothes, but I didn't actually *care* what they were wearing and I certainly didn't want anyone to feel like shit about herself for it. That might not make sense, but I truly thought I could crack a few jokes, help women shop for cute stuff, and send them on their way. Buh-bye! *What Not to Wear* and I didn't seem like a perfect match.

As I sat on the edge of my folding chair, my inner dialogue went something like this:

"Let's go, dipshit."

"No. We're staying."

"Shut up and get your ass out of this chair now."

"Nope. We promised the Universe we would stay."

"We lied."

"It wasn't a lie. We said we'd follow the Universe's guidance, no questions asked!"

"Fuck that. I'm outta here."

And so I got up from my chair, fully intending to leave and that's when the casting agent opened the door and called my name.

"Clinton Kelly?" she said.

And I replied, "That's me."

And she said, "Come on in."

And so I did. Interestingly, my mood changed the second I entered the casting room, from uncertainty to complete certainty that this was the most surreal experience I had had in forever. This was all happening so fast. Could this be the change I was looking for? Did anyone really think I was right for this job? Did I think I was right for this job?

About seven people sat in a line behind two rectangular tables that had been pushed together. Executives from the network (TLC), the production company (BBC), a camera operator, and Stacy London, whom I didn't even recognize from the video I had been watching in the waiting area because she was so casually dressed and wearing little, if any, makeup.

"Oh, hi," I said, when I realized it was her. "It's you." I waved and she waved back and smiled a big smile.

Someone asked me to take a seat, in a chair facing them all

like a firing squad. They asked me a bunch of questions, most of which I can't remember now. I do recall being asked which celebrity's style I admired, and I responded with the truth, that I really didn't care about celebrity style, because celebrities had stylists. It doesn't count when someone else is picking out your clothes.

I also remember that my mouth was really dry. Could it have been nerves? I don't recall being nervous.

"Can I have some water?" I asked, and started laughing.

"You want water?" a British woman named Abigail responded, as if nobody had ever asked her for water before.

"Yes," I said. "I'm all dry." My tongue seemed two sizes too big for my own mouth, which struck me as hysterical.

Everyone in the room laughed awkwardly and looked at me as though I were some sort of dry-mouthed lizard. Then someone had the idea of seating Stacy next to me and pointing a camera at the two of us as we flipped through entertainment magazines, ragging on some people and complimenting others. I really liked her. I had never met her before this day, and yet we chatted like two old friends for about half an hour, while everyone else in the room watched and laughed.

At one point I realized my hand was resting on Stacy's thigh. You might not know me as well as you think you do, Fanny. At the time, touching a relative stranger was very uncharacteristic of me.

I said, "I'm so sorry." And Stacy looked at me, puzzled.

"For what?" she asked.

"My hand is on your leg."

"Oh, God," she said. "I don't care." Then I felt kind of silly for bringing it up. But in some ways, I'm glad I did. I had forgotten about "me" for a moment and become "us."

I left that audition and by the next morning received a call to come back two days later, which was a Sunday, Father's Day, actually. I had been planning to go out to Long Island to visit my dad, so I called him and asked if it would be okay if he took a rain check. When I told him my reason for cancelling, he said, "Do what you gotta do, son. And knock 'em dead."

That audition would prove to be my final one. It was a miniversion of the show. They had whittled the field of what I was told were thousands of men down to two: me and someone else I never had the chance to meet. When I didn't hear from anyone for two weeks, I assumed they had chosen the other guy. And I was a little disappointed, but not devastated. Maybe because I never really wanted the job. The disappointment was more about having to figure out what the hell to do with my life. But TLC called me and offered me a five-year contract—their option to renew every year, not mine. I accepted, and that was that.

So, Fanny, does it sound like Fate muscled her way into a reality show casting? Or was it Destiny? Or perhaps it was Faith herself! My own Faith in the Universe, or some other higher power. I asked for a change, and it landed smack-dab in the middle of my flat-front-trousered lap. Fate, Faith, Destiny, Coincidence—who cares. The past is past, as they say. And I'm just plugging along in the present, the only way I know how, in a sense of amused wonderment at it all. Ever since I made a concerted effort to give up trying to determine *why* things happen, I've been a bit freer to experience things *when* they happen. Oh, here I go with that armchair philosophy again. Pay no attention to the musings of an old man like me.

Something tells me you want to know a little about my relationship with Stacy. What can I tell you about Ms. London, my cohost of ten years? She and I got along like . . . what's the expression? . . . a house on fire, from my first day on the job.

And as the years wore on, I often wished that house would have burned down to the ground.

We had an interesting relationship. Interesting to me, anyway, in the extremes I felt. For the first five years we worked together, I either adored her or despised her, and never anything in between, probably because we spent nearly sixty hours a week in captivity, rarely more than an arm's length away from each other. Trust me when I tell you that is just too much time to spend with any other human being you didn't choose of your own free will. And even then, it might be too much. We would occasionally joke that we were like a brother and sister trapped in the backseat during an excruciatingly long car trip. One minute wanting to play a game, the next wanting to kill the other for breathing. The last five years of the show, we settled into being "friends at work," which was considerably more peaceful.

Why did I love *and* loathe Stacy? I loved her, I think, because she's charming as hell. I've met few people so good as she at making others feel decidedly special. Also, she's got an amazing sense of humor. She cracked me up daily, even when I could barely stand the sight of her. Plus, she knows all the words to *A Chorus Line*. I mean, how could I not adore someone who wants to sing "Dance Ten, Looks Three" with me upward of thirty times a day? We were two well-intentioned warriors, traveling the country attempting to convince women, one at a time, that perhaps, despite everything they had been told by abusive ex-boyfriends, bullying classmates, even well-intentioned mothers, they did deserve to feel pretty. Some believed us. Some were damaged enough to know that a good bra and platform pumps would not come close to repairing their souls.

I loathed Stacy because . . . well . . . maybe there was some jealousy on my part. She really seemed to enjoy, nay, need the attention of others, and I felt that she was almost constantly jockeying for it. For that reason, and perhaps others, she received more attention than I did. Even though I rarely wanted attention—that's the truth if you care to believe it—I found myself continually annoyed that she did. I was perfectly content with our own little system of two. Us against them! But she needed more, and then I grew to want more too.

Oh, there's more to our relationship than that, Fanny, but I'm getting a headache just unpacking it. I'll say this, though, before I move on: there's a part of me that will love Stacy London forever, and a part of me that would be just fine if I never saw her again for the rest of my life. We had great chemistry, for sure. But just like when you combine baking soda and vinegar, after the fun part fizzles out, you're left with a puddle of nothing in particular.

The show made me rich, so that's nice. Not filthy rich, but I'm doing okay. I doubt I would have made as much money had I continued chugging along in my magazine editing career. I'm thankful for that, and for having a job that makes some people smile or think or both. And for the people who came into my life because of the show. Out of the three-hundred-plus "contributors" as we called them, the people who agreed to televised makeovers, I still keep in touch with about a hundred of them, some more than others, of course, and probably another fifty people who worked on the series—various producers, crew members, wardrobe assistants, makeup artists. Sometimes I can't believe I'm the same painfully shy guy who had a total of seven friends, give or take a few based on the collective mood, in high school. Life sure is fucking weird, Fanny.

When *What Not to Wear* ended a few years ago, many reporters asked me about my favorite and least favorite makeovers and the worst fashion faux pas I had ever witnessed. But not a single one asked me what I had learned about women over ten years of listening to their concerns about their bodies and their clothes. I'll tell you what has stuck with me the most, Fanny, because I think you of all people might actually be curious.

Women want to feel beautiful. I've never met one who said she didn't, and believe me, I've asked around. (I sometimes wonder if, similarly, all men yearn to be handsome, but I'll admit to being far less intrigued by what's going on between the ears of the males of our species.) To my point, American society has clearly learned how to capitalize on the desire of women to be desired, with billions of dollars spent each year on diet books, cosmetics, hair products, apparel, plastic surgery, the whole she-bang. I certainly don't think any of those categories is inherently evil—not evil at all, actually. In fact, I'm a big fan.

The problem, as far as I can tell, is that women spend infinitely more time than men paying attention to, competing with, worrying about, *everyone other than themselves.*

Sometimes I just want to shake you by the shoulders, Fanny, and tell you to stop surrendering your power, because that's what you're doing. Every single time you set up a comparison between yourself and someone else, YOU LOSE, NO ONE WINS. Chrissy Teigen has beautiful hair . . . that has nothing whatsoever to do with *you.* Jennifer Lawrence has perfect skin . . . that does not involve *you.* Kim Kardashian's ass . . . should arouse absolutely no feelings in you concerning your own ass!

And the more you keep comparing, the less your own beauty becomes self-evident. Just because you're not a super-model, movie star, or Instagram celebrity does not mean that your beauty is any less important than anyone else's. Sure, it's OK to look, even admire, just be careful when comparing apples to oranges. (Apple: You getting yourself ready for work in the morning. Orange: Woman who has paid a stylist, personal chef, trainer, lighting director, and photo editor to help her post "selfies.")

Start focusing on you, Fanny, your power, your value, the stuff that goes way deeper than designer jeans and the perfect shade of lipstick. But also on the perfect shade of lipstick if that makes you happy. Because you deserve to be happy. I am certain of little in this world, but I am certain about that.

I'll bring this letter to its inevitable close now. Thank you for reading this far, and for watching. I'm still no closer to knowing whether *What Not to Wear* was an act of Fate, a brush with Destiny, a kick in the pants from the Universe, or just a lucky break. But it's fascinating, isn't it, that my request to be pointed in the "right direction" led you and me together in some small, I hope not insignificant, way. I still don't know who you are, but I'm glad you're out there.

Stay fabulous,

Clinton

MEMORIZING PORN

When Mr. Berry, our tenth-grade biology teacher, plopped a formaldehyde-soaked fetal pig on an aluminum tray at our shared lab station, Lisa and I looked at each other with sad eyes and morbid smiles. It looked like a small hairless dog with skin the color of lunch meat. "Oy. Look at that face," Lisa said, channeling Jackie Mason. "It's a face only a mother could love. I was hoping he'd become a doctor. Such a disappointment. You're dead to me." She fake-spat on the floor.

I burst out laughing. Her old-Jewish-man shtick always cracked me up.

Lisa had moved from a nearby town into my school district in the middle of seventh grade and, because her last name began with an H and mine with a K, she was placed in my homeroom. *That's tough*, I remember thinking, *making new friends in junior high*. Because of my parents' divorce, I had changed schools a few times over the past four years and hated it every time. Inevitably, I would vomit before my first day of school and occasionally sob afterward.

So I looked right at the new girl and smiled. She smiled back, but not in the self-conscious or defensively bitchy style of other girls her age. It was a look I hadn't seen before, expressing a combination of boredom, mischief, and omnipotence. Somehow she seemed both above and below it all, like she knew this whole adolescence thing was pure bullshit but found it amusing anyway. We became best friends almost immediately and here we were three years later laying a guilt trip on an unborn pig.

"You're worse than dead to me. You're unkosher."

Mr. Berry, clad in black elbow-length gloves that might have been elegant had they not been made of rubber, was doling out more to-be-dissected specimens. He turned his head back toward us and said, "If you don't laugh, you'll cry." It was his favorite expression. His Maine accent, much different from the Long Island ones we grew up among, made almost everything he said sound hilarious to us. Except that line. He was right, and we knew it.

"Let's name him Abercrombie," I whispered. For some reason I had become obsessed with a commercial for laundry detergent in which a dutiful mother attempts to save a grass-stained day by breaking out a jug of All. This delights her precocious children, who see this as an opportunity to familiarize their Labrador puppy with the alphabet. "Let's teach Abercrombie how to spell!" one of them suggests, while the other glides the dog's paw over the letters on the bottle. "A-L-L!"

Lisa agreed that the name suited him and over the course of the next week, we cut into Abercrombie with our scalpels, learning about various organs and systems, all the while pretending he was our own flesh and blood.

"Look at our baby's intestines," we would say. "So curly, like his mother's."

"Oh, his heart is smaller than I thought, just like his daddy's." And every day we would teach him a new word, moving his little pig foot along imaginary letters. On Monday: "Let's teach Abercrombie how to spell! P-E-N-I-S."

On Tuesday: "V-A-G-I-N-A."

On Wednesday: "T-H-R-E-E-W-A-Y."

On Thursday: "E-J-A-C-U-L-A-T-E."

Lisa cut biology on Friday, which was disappointing. We were scheduled to dissect Abercrombie's brain. And teach him to spell "anal beads."

Skipping class had become a common occurrence for Lisa. Her mother had been battling breast cancer for a few years, and under the not-so-watchful eye of her father, Lisa was living a life apparently devoid of rules and goals. So Lisa became a little bit of a wild child before my eyes, which fascinated the hell out of me. My life was crammed so full of parentally imposed rules and self-imposed goals I could hardly breathe. I didn't even know there was another way to live.

Sometimes I'd stop by Lisa's house and stand in awe at the condition of her bedroom: clothes on the floor piled as high as the bed. Half-full mugs on her dresser with little circles of bluish-green mold floating like miniature galaxies in a coffee-beige cosmos. I might spot a month-old newspaper lying next to her pillow or a bikini top hanging from the doorknob in the middle of February.

If my room looked like this, I thought, *Mike and Terri would each shit a ten-pound brick.* The most nonnegotiable edict in our house was to never, ever, under any circumstances leave it without making your bed. When I would sassily ask what difference it made, Terri would say, "Because I might have someone over while you're at school," which of course made me wonder who was visiting my mother during the school day and why the hell was she showing them my bedroom? When I asked, she never answered.

Was she showing the house to prospective buyers? ("This room is perfect for a teenage boy with an Olivia Newton-John obsession.") Was she having an affair? ("I force my children to make their beds. Does that turn you on?") Was she giving tours to Japanese sightseers? ("In America, we value . . . discipline.") The whole thing seemed pretty illogical, but she wouldn't budge.

Thirty years later, bed-making is a popular topic around our Christmas dinner table. My sisters and I laugh at my parents' obsession and reminisce about our individual ways of coping with it: I used to make my bed the second I arose from it to avoid any confrontation whatsoever. Jodi would leave the house, somehow "forgetting" to make her bed, and return home to an apoplectic Terri nearly every day. And Courtney, the twisted genius she is, would sleep on *top* of her fully made bed, covering herself with a blanket, then shove that blanket under the bed first thing in the morning.

The only respite I received from the barrage of rules and chores—making my bed, vacuuming the house, doing my own laundry, taking out the trash, being home by ten—was when I went to work. Even more important to my parents than keeping a tidy house was making money, and I had scored a job as a busboy in the nicest restaurant in town, Danfords Inn. While most kids my age were earning minimum wage working at one of the many fast-food chains nearby, I was bringing home a hundred bucks a night in cash tips.

So I was excused from family excursions to the ski slopes of Vermont in the winter and the beaches of Fire Island in the summer. We were living pretty high on the hog at the time, thanks to Mike's beauty-supply business. Formerly a hairstylist, he made what turned out to be a wise career move, from giving individual women perms to selling salons the chemicals required to cre-

ate truly huge hair. Considering we lived in the perm capital of
the world (Long Island) in the heyday of the perm (the 1980s),
I thought we should have been living in a castle instead of a
split-level ranch. But I didn't complain. We had a ski house and
a boat, and I had my teenage privacy for most of the weekend
while the rest of the family was gone.

During the weekends I had the house to myself, Lisa and I
developed a private routine, separate from the weekday customs
(mostly of eating fast food) we engaged in with our friend Meredith. The three of us were a trio, brought together by drama club
and chorus class. In our firmly middle-class school district, those
activities didn't make us too popular, but we weren't pariahs either.
Mostly we spun in our own clique, a satellite too small to be noticed
by the jocks and cheerleaders who lived squarely in the center of the
universe. I resented our fringe status more than I dared admit, but
not enough to attend even a single football game in four years.

Meredith, Lisa, and I had several nicknames for one another.
On any given day, Meredith would be referred to as Bonnie,
Snap, or The Superego. I would be Clyde, Crackle, or The
Ego. And Lisa would be Baby Face, Pop, or The Id. Lisa always
seemed to end up with the punchiest nicknames of the three of
us, but neither Meredith nor I seemed to mind because, out of
the group, Lisa was the one most likely to flash her tits at a passing car or scream "I just found my G-spot!" in a crowded movie
theater. She earned them.

Like any triad, we occasionally split into twos. Sometimes
Lisa and Meredith would get together alone and do girl things,
like shop for homecoming dresses. (I was uninterested at the
time, which seems funny in hindsight.) Sometimes Meredith
and I would get together for coffee at the diner and study for a
Regent's exam. (Lisa had zero intention of going to college.) And

every Saturday Lisa and I would get together, just the two of us, and memorize porn like a couple of pervert savants.

So, every weekend, I would work in the restaurant on Friday night, the rest of the family having left for a weekend trip around three o'clock, and come home to a house empty except for Noel, our eczematous Lhasa Apso. I'd let the dog out in the backyard to relieve herself, grab a few leftover chicken cutlets from the fridge, and watch TV until I fell asleep on the couch with Noel at my feet. I would sleep until around ten the next morning, feed the dog, and call Lisa. She would always be the one to answer her house phone because she slept with it next to her bed.

"Hello," she'd growl.

"Did I wake you?"

"Of course you woke me. You ask me that same damn question every Saturday."

"What time does the video store open?"

She let out an annoyed groan. "Oh my God. Eleven. It opens at eleven, just like every other fucking Saturday."

"Great. So I'll pick you up at eleven," I'd say. "We'll get there around eleven ten. We don't want to seem too eager." She hung up without replying, but I knew she'd be ready on time.

At 10:59 I would get in my car, a 1979 Chevy Blazer my parents gave me after they were done with it. The car was basically a tank—an SUV before everyone started driving SUVs—that would break down almost weekly and cost me a full weekend's worth of tips to repair. Lisa lived around the block, so I could arrive at her house at 11:00 on the dot and honk the horn. A few minutes later, she would emerge from her front door, looking perturbed as usual. She was a little wisp of a thing, five feet tall, probably not even a hundred pounds, with a mane of chestnut hair half-assedly feathered because she just rolled out of bed.

"Hey Clyde," she said, lifting herself into the passenger seat. Today she wore acid-washed jeans, white sneakers, and an over-sized lemon-yellow sweater.

"Good morning, Baby Face," I replied.

Lisa and I drove to the video store where Lisa's father had a membership he never used. Located in a strip mall featuring a Carvel and my dentist's office, it was one of those independently run shops that were eventually crushed by Blockbuster, which was in turn crushed by the Internet.

The store was pretty big as far as stores of its kind went; the space had previously been a bank so it featured a drive-through window, which I always thought was pretty cool. But because the store wasn't even computerized, the interaction at the window was inevitably more time-consuming than just getting out of your car and walking in. In any case, our video-selection process was more nuanced than asking a dim-witted teller for a recommendation.

We entered—just your average teenage duo looking for a movie to pass some time on an average Saturday in an average one-horse town—and started picking up VHS boxes. Younger readers might not understand how the video-rental process worked back then, so allow me to explain. A local store might have multiple freestanding racks and shelves displaying empty video boxes, which you could pick up to read a description of the movie and see a few stills. Usually, if you wanted to rent that particular movie, you would bring the box up to the cashier, who would give you the VHS tape to take with you in a generic hard plastic case. But this particular store had a particularly high-tech Velcro tab selection feature: When you decided upon a movie to rent, you would remove the corresponding "button," a metal rim tab about the size of a quarter with the movie's name written in felt-tip marker on the front and a Velcro button on the back, and bring that to the cashier. Ridiculous, I know. But at least we could watch TV without having to get up to change the channel.

We began perusing the racks, beginning with the movies closest to the front door.

Lisa picked up *The Shining*. "This looks like fun."

"Nah. I hate romantic comedies," I replied. I held up *Raiders of the Lost Ark*. "What about this one?"

"No. I hate arks."

The bit continued for half an hour, same as every week. We were "That Crazy Couple Who Can't Decide on a Movie," all for the sake of the pimply-faced clerk two years our senior who barely noticed our existence. You would need a time-lapse camera to even realize it was happening, but the entire time we were slowly making our way to the back of the store.

Because that's where the "adult" room was.

Eventually, Lisa would feign complete exasperation and say, "I can't find anything I want to watch. Maybe there's something in this back room." Then she'd skip through the swinging saloon-style doors into The Room of Porn.

At this point my heart was beating like a jackhammer in my scrawny rib cage, but sensing the clerk's eyes on me, I picked up another movie. "How about *Annie*? I like the part where the aliens kill everyone."

"Get in here," Lisa barked in her most annoyed voice. And as though I were jumping into an ice-cold pool, I held my breath and pushed myself through just one side of the swinging doors, so as not to cause too much swinging.

The Room of Porn was windowless and fluorescently lit, about ten feet square with five levels of shelves on all sides, every inch of which was lined with box covers. It was like being in a candy store, except this candy gave you hard-ons instead of cavities. I felt dizzy, probably because blood had been diverted from my brain. My instinct was to just grab any one of the Velcro buttons and get the hell out, but that's not the way Lisa worked.

"This one is fine." I held out *On Golden Blonde*.

She wasn't looking at me. She was reading the cover of *The Poonies*. "Cool your jets," she said. "I want to find one with a nice story."

"Look at this. It's called *Beverly Hills Cox*. I'm guessing it's about horny policemen in California."

"Shhhhhhh!" She was reading about the plot of *Wet Paint*, the story of a horny artist in California.

Back then porn was pretty silly, not the gonzo stuff you can't avoid today. The average porno movie was about an hour and a half, with a story line, often a parody of a popular TV show or movie, and sometimes snappy dialogue. There were costume changes and sets and awesomely cheesy background music made on a synthesizer in some guy's mother's basement. The really high-end stuff featured actual theme songs.

After another half hour, Lisa and I were able to agree on *Caddy Shack Up*, the story of horny caddies in California.

"OK," I said, pulling some money out of my jeans. "Here's a twenty. I'll meet you in the car." She rolled her eyes, but she knew the drill.

I left The Room of Porn through one of the swinging doors. As per our unspoken agreement, Lisa would wait another five minutes before emerging. During that time I would pick up a few more video boxes from the nonporn collection and act as though I still couldn't decide on one, slowly making my way toward the front of the store, at which point I would let out a sigh of defeat and give a shrug of indecision. Then I'd head out into the parking lot and wait for Lisa.

I decided to grab a soft-serve from Carvel before getting in the Blazer. Lisa was taking forever. I had finished almost the entire vanilla cone with chocolate sprinkles by the time she arrived.

"What took you so long?"

"Ronald was there."

"Who?" I was wrapping the last bit of the cone in a paper napkin to give to Noel.

"My father, you idiot."

"Oh my God. In the porno section?"

"No. He was at the drive-through returning some movies. I almost shit my pants."

I laughed like it was the funniest thing I had heard in my life.

"Let's go to Wendy's, asshole," Lisa said. "I think Meredith's working."

High on the excitement of a new dirty movie to watch tonight and the freedom of having my entire house to ourselves, we drove toward Nesconset Highway where a Wendy's, Taco Bell, McDonald's, Dunkin' Donuts, and Ground Round peacefully coexisted within a quarter mile of one another. When "Never Gonna Let You Go" by Sergio Mendez came on the radio, we blasted it and sang along at full voice.

Lisa had been correct. Meredith was working, but not the register as she usually did. She was at the griddle, so she didn't notice us when we got in line to order. She took her job of flipping burgers very seriously, and her manager, a nervous-looking man of around thirty, was flitting around nearby.

"What do you think of that guy?" asked Lisa, referring to the manager.

"He looks like a rapist," I said. "Why?"

Lisa let out a snort. "Awesome. Meredith has the hots for him."

"Gross. He's so old."

"I know, right? I wouldn't be surprised if she lost the big V to him."

"No way," I said. "Meredith will be a virgin until her wedding night."

"Oh, please. Nobody waits that long anymore."

"I'm going to," I said.

"That's so romantic." Lisa rolled her eyes. "If you ask me, they should do it over there on the salad bar, right between the croutons and the shredded carrots."

"That doesn't seem very hygienic. Or comfortable. What's his name?" I asked.

"Mark. As in Mark my word, he's gonna pop her cherry tomato."

My laugh caught Meredith's attention. She must have been able to sense our mood because she shot us a look that threatened retribution for any behavior that might embarrass her, which Lisa took as a challenge, of course. When we ordered our food from the cashier, whom we did not know, Lisa asked to speak to the manager. The cashier grabbed Mark by the elbow, and Meredith glared at us. Mark hung a basket of French fries to drain and approached the counter.

"Can I help you?" he asked.

"Yes," Lisa said. "I was wondering, is the bleu cheese fresh?"

"Is it *fresh*?" Evidently, it was not a question he received often.

"Yes, fresh."

He spoke as one might to an eight-year-old. "It's salad dressing. And it comes in a large plastic tub."

"Thank you," Lisa said, "I will take that into consideration." Mark returned to salting his fries.

After I paid for lunch, we sat at a table by the window, not far from the salad bar. I scarfed down my chicken sandwich and saw Meredith enter the dining room through the door marked EMPLOYEES ONLY behind Lisa. "Uh-oh," I said. "She looks pissed."

"We didn't do anything wrong," Lisa stated.

Mark must have put Meredith on tray duty because she began to tidy the empty tables around us. She wouldn't look in our direction, and I couldn't blame her. We followed her with our eyes. Once she had a few trays stacked in her hands, she passed by our table.

"You guys are such assholes," she said.

"I didn't do anything," I blurted, as she made her way back to the kitchen.

"You are such a pussy," Lisa said to me, through a bite of half-chewed hamburger.

I shrugged. Maybe I was. I felt bad for laughing at Meredith's expense, but I was also kind of hurt that she had a secret crush she had only shared with Lisa. We were a trio. If I had been a girl, Meredith would have told me too.

We finished lunch in relative silence, and I dropped Lisa off at home. I gave her my house key and told her I'd be home around midnight. I went home, entering through the garage, and put the porno in my dresser beneath my underwear, just in case there was an emergency and my parents came home while I was gone. I couldn't have *Caddy Shack Up* lying on the kitchen counter. I also took a bottle of champagne, one of the many Mike's clients had given him around Christmas, from the back of the liquor cabinet and put it in the refrigerator. Mike and Terri would never miss it. I had never seen them drink champagne in the seven or so years they had been together.

* * *

Work was uneventful, just the usual filling of water glasses, folding of napkins, clearing of tables, setting of tables, emptying of
ashtrays. I was actually an excellent busboy. The restaurant had
recently held a competition for head busboy, which I won, so I
made an extra dollar per hour and got the busiest stations, the
ones with the best view of the harbor outside. The waitresses all
liked me because if I ever saw them so much as lift an empty plate,
I would swoop in and finish the job. If they told me table 12
needed more breadsticks, I was on it like fire. They were obligated
to give me 15 percent of their tips, but most gave me 20. Occasionally a diner, usually a man on a date with a woman, would
tip me directly, thanking me for taking good care of them. I loved
that job. It was the one place I felt I was truly popular.

I returned home around twelve thirty to see Lisa's car in the
driveway.

"This dog has been scaring the crap out of me," she
announced when I walked in the door. She was sitting downstairs in our den watching TV with Noel on her lap. "She's been
growling at every little noise outside. I thought someone was out
there trying to kill us."

"She's a pain in the ass like that," I said. "Last weekend I
barely slept because she was barking at the bedroom window at
three a.m. Lhasas were imperial guard dogs in Tibet or some shit
like that."

"Thanks for the history lesson, dork. Where's the movie?"

"In my underwear drawer. Can you get the champagne out
of the fridge? I'll set up the movie."

Lisa went up to the kitchen, and I rushed upstairs to change
out of my uniform into jeans and a polo shirt. Soon, she came
downstairs with the bottle and three brown ceramic coffee mugs,
one of which was to be used as an ashtray. We were one of the

first families on our block to have a big-screen TV, which was housed in a giant wooden cabinet that took up half the room. As she poured us each a mug of champagne, I put the video in the VCR and hit PLAY on the remote.

Lisa sat on the couch, and I sat on the floor. We watched the entire movie from start to finish in engrossed silence. Neither of us spoke. Neither of us took eyes from the screen for one second. We sipped champagne and refilled our mugs without looking at them. We lit, smoked, and extinguished cigarettes without looking at them. We were taking it all in, every sexual act, moan, and groan. But mostly we were memorizing the dialogue.

Like clockwork, when the movie ended, I hit rewind. The tape whirred in the machine and abruptly stopped. I hit PLAY again, and we began our second viewing of the evening, this time repeating all the dialogue we could remember and voicing our critiques. Such was our creative process.

Caddy Shack Up is the story of Cathy, an attractive young woman with a slightly crooked front tooth and shockingly conical nipples, who takes a job as a caddy at the Burning Bush Golf Club. In the first scene, we learn that while she would be open to meeting and marrying a rich club member, she is also just plain happy using her body for sexual pleasure. "You don't have to have an alterior motive for everything," says Cathy. To which Lisa cried: "The word is *ulterior*, you illiterate skank. Not *alterior*. *Ulterior*."

Cathy is soon undressed at the hands of a more experienced female caddy who says, "Why don't you just lay down here and I'll show you my specialty—the club massage."

"What is with these people?" I wondered aloud. "You want her to lie there, not lay there. Lie means to recline. Lay means to place. I have never been so disappointed in the American educational system. Canadians must watch this stuff and laugh at us."

"Well, they are the superior race."

The second scene was our favorite for its pure absurdity and aggressive sex. It featured Sam, played by some catfishy mustachioed guy in a royal blue polo shirt (identical to the one I had just changed into!), and an actress named Purple Passion, who quickly became our hero. She was black and spoke with an exotic accent (which I recently learned was from Baltimore). They were in the clubhouse bar and Purple Passion was putting the moves on him. Sam started off the scene by mumbling, "Hellacious caddy, hellacious caddy."

"What the fuck does that even mean?" Lisa asked.

"He's setting the scene, letting us all know what a bad caddy she is, which does seem like a mean thing to say while she's rubbing all up against him."

"Prick."

Then we had to stop the tape and rewind it a few times because we couldn't understand what Sam was saying. It took us a solid ten minutes to determine that he had muttered: "I like to putt with holes this stiff."

"That doesn't make any sense," Lisa said. "He must've screwed up his line. It was probably, I like to putt with *poles* this stiff. Not *holes*."

"You don't putt with a golf *pole*. You putt with a putter."

"Who cares? I hate golf, and this guy is obviously drunk."

Sam and Purple get down to business, despite the fact that Lisa and I agreed Purple Passion could have scored a better-looking dude. She seemed like the type of girl we could hang out with, if there were any black kids at our school. Everyone we knew was Italian, Jewish, or Puerto Rican. A black porn star friend would have been fun.

While she's having sex with the drunk golfer, apropos of

absolutely nothing, Purple Passion declares: "It's not me knowin' the clubs, it's me havin' the body."

This line outraged Lisa so much that she demanded I stop the tape.

"What's your problem?" I asked.

"She missed her opportunity for the best line in this whole stupid movie! She should have said, 'It's not me knowin' the clubs, it's me knowin' the *strokes*!'"

"Yes!" I yelled, startling the dog, who up until this point had been asleep, despite all the sex noises blaring from the TV. "It's not me knowin' the clubs, it's me knowin' the strokes! Of course! I just fucking love you."

It was true. I did love her, not in any sort of romantic way, but for her wit and her grumpiness and her loyalty and her dependability. She was The Id, and I was The Ego. And tonight we were operating free of The Superego, who was probably fast asleep in her bed, dreaming of making sweet love to a nervous-looking man with glasses on a bed of iceberg lettuce. Or romaine, which would be fancier.

Lisa went home after we finished watching the movie for the second time. Cathy the Caddy thinks about quitting, but then she decides not to. That's the entire plot. I told Lisa I would return the tape on my way to work the brunch shift the next morning.

"Give me one ring when you get home so I know you're not dead," I told her.

Lisa rolled her eyes.

But a few minutes later, the phone rang once, and I curled up on the couch where she had been sitting, shut off the lights, and fell asleep.

TURD IN THE PUNCHBOWL

Had I known when my alarm rang that Paula Deen was going to ruin my Wednesday, I probably would have just said fuck it and gone back to bed.

"Oh, my Goddddd," I groaned. "I'm so *tiiiiired*." It was 6:15, about the same time I wake up every morning, give or take fifteen minutes. Usually, I spring out of bed with considerable energy, the source of which mystifies me, but not today. Mary had kept me up half the night by wedging herself right up against my kidneys.

Damon was already awake; he had an early patient. "I was waiting for your alarm to go off so I could make coffee," he said.

In normal living conditions, at least in Western society, one half of a couple can make coffee in the morning without waking the other, but when we renovated our apartment I had the brilliant idea of configuring it as one big, open space. "We're going to honor the architectural history of the neighborhood and create an authentic Tribeca loft," I had told anyone who would listen. "The bed will be right smack in the middle of the room. It's going to be superchic."

Five years later I want to kick myself in the nuts for sounding like a pretentious asshole. I just hope that eventually we can sell it to another pretentious asshole for three times what we paid for it. But because of the floor plan—which is *no* floor plan—Damon and I need to be on the same sleep schedule, lest one of us do something ridiculous like open the refrigerator and shine the light in the other's slumbering face.

The coffeemaker, one of those all-in-one numbers that grinds beans, brews espresso, and steams milk, roared and hissed. A few minutes later, latte in hand, Damon sat at the foot of the bed. "Bad night's sleep?" he asked.

"Yeah, thanks to this pain in the ass," I answered, referring to Mary, who was listening intently. "Do you see how much room she's taking up? I'm literally hanging off the side of the bed." I wasn't exaggerating. My left arm and shoulder were off the mattress.

"You know, you can train her to sleep on the floor," he said.

"No, I can't, Damon," I said, enunciating both syllables of his name. "She's been sleeping in our bed for the last seven years. What's she gonna think when all of a sudden we just throw her on the floor? I'll tell you what she's gonna think: She's gonna think we don't love her anymore and then she'll get depressed and wish she was never born."

Damon told me I was projecting. Or anthropomorphizing. Maybe both. I don't know. I kind of zoned out, as I usually do at this point in this particular conversation. See, most of the time I enjoy being married to a psychologist. Damon is the most thoughtful, kind, supportive, introspective man I have ever met. When we argue, which is rarely, I find myself saying things like, "I'm sorry for acting out, but I'm frustrated by the events of the day," or "Let's step back and examine our rage for a moment."

It's actually kind of amazing. But when Damon has the audacity to imply that my relationship with Mary is slightly cuckoo, I want to rip out a chunk of his perfect hair.

I'm not an idiot. I know everyone thinks Mary is a dog. And she may very well be, but there's also a very distinct possibility, as far as I'm concerned, that she's a human being trapped in a thirteen-pound Jack Russell terrier's body, albeit a human being who's obsessed with smelling random puddles of piss on the sidewalk. And so I give her everything she could ever need to live an emotionally fulfilling life: organic freeze-dried chicken, filtered water, treats baked in small batches by local artisans, weekend hikes on the Appalachian Trail, spa days, et cetera.

"You're right," I said. "I'm just being silly. I'll start training Mary to sleep in her own bed tonight." All three of us know I am lying through my porcelain-veneered teeth.

I gently rubbed Mary's velvety belly, wrested myself from bed, and shuffled across the concrete floors toward the bathroom, where the morning's clothes awaited me. I had laid them on the vanity the night before with the intention of leaving for work as quickly as possible. Since the renovation, I've learned how to get ready for work in just fifteen minutes. Of course it helps that ABC employs a team of people to dress and groom me. I'm really only responsible for brushing my own teeth and maintaining my private parts. They do the rest!

I left the apartment after kissing Damon and Mary goodbye on their mouths. Damon insists I do it in that order for sanitary reasons, though I suspect it's a hierarchy thing. As per our usual arrangement, he will drop Mary off at the sitter on his way to work. Heading to the subway, I stopped by my favorite coffee shop and ordered a flat white for my walk. It's a few short blocks away and usually the most tranquil part of my day. At this time of year, the sun and streetlamps halfheartedly compete to illuminate the sidewalks, pigeons coo from window ledges above, and deliverymen unload palettes of bread from big square trucks. Even the 1 train provides a sense of calm this early. A tacit understanding exists among the burly construction men, dozing hospital workers, bankers, and myself: Let's start this day in peace.

In my orange plastic seat, I opened my e-mail to read the itinerary my assistant, Jackie, sent me the night before.

Wednesday, March 11, 2015

<u>7:30 a.m.</u>
Call time at *The Chew*.

Production meeting.

Rehearsal.

Hair, makeup, wardrobe.

<u>8:45 a.m.</u>
Shoot Episode #756 "*The Chew*'s Spring Break!"

Airs same day. You're making your macadamia-crusted chicken with mango and pineapple salsa in segments 2 and 3.

Guest: Paula Deen. She's cooking with Michael Symon later in the show.

<u>9:45 a.m.</u>
Meet with Jennifer re: upcoming interview with Mekhi Phifer. Meet with Katie re upcoming cocktail segment. Meet with Brad re: upcoming Clinton's Craft Corner.

11:00 a.m.
Production meeting.

Rehearsal.

Hair and makeup touch-ups. Change wardrobe.

12:15 p.m.
Shoot *The Chew*, Episode #759 "Fast 'n' Fresh."

Air Date: 3/16/15 (You don't have much to do in this show, but Alonna and her sister will be in the audience.)

1:15 p.m.
Wrap *The Chew*.

2:00 p.m.
Stop by office.

Pay bills.

Post on Facebook and Twitter about new web content.

Meet with Jill re: Macy's Orange County event.

Call Kate to discuss styling for new TLC show.

SIGN INCOME TAX EXTENSION FORMS!

4:00 p.m.
Workout.

6:00 p.m.
Dinner with Emily (You put this in the calendar yourself. Do you need me to make reservations somewhere?)

9:00 p.m.
Pick up dog from sitter.

The day appeared to be rather typical, though my eyes did hover for an extra half second on Paula Deen's name, just enough time for a quick flutter of dread to wash over me. Nothing too ill-boding, more like the kind of feeling you get when you're reminded that later in the day you have an appointment for your annual prostate exam.

I've never really been a fan of Paula's, but that's the way life is. Maybe her essence whispers sweet nothings to your very soul. I, however, find her shtick more annoying than a hangnail. And just for the record, it's not about her Southern heritage or Southern food in general, because I'm quite fond of many Southern people and Southern food can be freakin' delicious. Before I met Paula, my distaste for her was probably due to her seeming, in my opinion, very one-note—*and that note is butter, y'all!* Then I met her in person during the *The Chew*'s first season and, while I really wanted to like the woman, her good old-fashioned "charm" struck me as completely artificial. Then came her N-word scandal, and after that she admitted to her fans that she had Type 2 diabetes—two years after her doctors diagnosed her but only after securing a lucrative diabetes drug contract, and in the interim continuing to push an unhealthy lifestyle. So, eh, I'm not a fan. And I get the feeling she knows it.

I have little, if any, say regarding the guests who appear on *The Chew* because I am a host and not a producer. And even though I like the show's producers very much, they have a history with Paula, having produced her show on Food Network for many years. So when she's booked on the show, I say hello and welcome her with as much enthusiasm as I can muster. That's what I'm paid to do and I do it relatively convincingly.

Today Paula made her entrance in the second-to-last segment of the show, teaming up with Michael Symon to demonstrate her recipe for chicken wings, while I sat nearby with my other cohosts, Daphne Oz, Carla Hall, and Mario Batali. When it comes to presenting a recipe clearly and efficiently, Michael is quite possibly the best in the business, but the interaction I witnessed between him and Paula made absolutely no sense. He might as well have been interviewing a crack-smoking unicorn about how to make a rainbow sandwich. Seriously. I knew *less* about how to make chicken wings *after* Paula's demo than I did before it even began, which means she was actually able to destroy existing neural pathways in my brain pertaining to the effects of heat on poultry.

During the commercial break, our off-camera kitchen team placed a huge platter piled with three different types of goo-covered chicken wings on the table in front of the hosts. Evidently, this was the finished product of all that nonsense, as if somehow during the three minutes between segments, Paula magically became lucid and just whipped up lunch for thirty people.

"What's on these things?" I asked Daphne, who sat next to me. "I don't know what the hell just happened."

"Me either," she said. "I think the pile on the right is peanut butter and jelly sauce. The ones on the left have green pepper jelly. The ones in the middle . . . I have no idea."

I rolled my eyes. I was experiencing one of those very rare moments when I didn't like my job but—and I want to make this very clear—knew that in the grand scheme of things it was really no big fucking deal. I wasn't banging rocks in a diamond mine. I wasn't brokering a peace deal between the Koreas. I wasn't administering the polio vaccine to poor kids in Appalachia. My job was to smile for the camera and eat a goddamn piece of chicken. And I had every intention of doing just that.

As the commercial break ended and Michael reintroduced Paula to the viewing audience, I speared a wing off the platter with my fork and put it on the small plate in front of me. And after using my knife to scrape off, as discreetly as possible, some of the green pepper jelly sauce, I realized I had a crucial decision to make: Should I cut the meat off the chicken wing and bring it to my mouth *with the fork I'm already holding*? Or should I put down the fork and knife and eat the wing with my fingers, which as we know is the usual and accepted method of eating chicken wings in the United States of America.

I was at a fork in the road with a fork in my hand.

Screw it, I thought. I'll just quickly put some of this chicken in my mouth . . . with a fork.

Well, that didn't escape the preternaturally blue-eyed gaze of Miss Paula Deen. "What are you *doin'*," she drawl-screeched, "eatin' that with a *fork and knife*?!?"

Oh, for Christ's sake.

Rather than explain my reasoning—the fork was in my hand, the wings had too much sauce, it was nine thirty in the morning, and these wings are about as appealing to me as a shit sandwich—I decided to laugh it off.

"Who, me?" I joked, dropping my utensils and picking up the wing with my fingers. It's just the easiest way out, I figured. I'll laugh at myself, and she'll stop acting like she's Blanche DuBois who just walked in on Stanley Kowalski dipping his dick in the lemonade.

But she didn't drop it. She exclaimed on live-to-tape television, "You look like the turd in the punchbowl!"

That fucking bitch, I thought. What I wanted to say was: *You're a guest on the show I cohost, a national network daytime talk show watched by about 3 million people a day, including my husband, friends, parents, and grandparents, serving me the most revolting thing I've had to eat in years, and you have enough rocks in your ball sack to call me a* turd. *If I had any pull whatsoever on this show, your ass would never be on it.* But I'm a professional, so I said, "I've been called worse by better."

It was partially true. I have been called worse. Much worse. But not necessarily by anyone better. And certainly not on television.

The show ended a few minutes later, and I waved a quick good-bye to the studio audience. I usually shake a few hands and take a few photos to show my appreciation for their attendance, but I was too furious to interact with strangers. So I detached my microphone and headed to my dressing room.

We shot the next show a few hours later, which was completely uneventful. Except for my terse exchange with Paula, the workday was the kind I forget about immediately upon leaving the studio. But I was in a foul mood, so I decided to ask my friend Emily if she would take a rain check for dinner. She did. I went to my meetings and my workout, and as I exited the gym, I received a text from Damon: "Do you want to grab dinner?"

"I can meet you at Odeon in ten minutes," I answered.

"Perfect! See you there."

I arrived first and the hostess, a very chic woman named Roya, led me to a table in the corner. I ordered a French 75, a delicious combination of gin, lemon juice, sugar, and champagne, which is named for a World War I gun famous for its ability to fire shrapnel. Damon walked in shortly thereafter, looking as handsome as a man can, in a gray tweed sport coat with elbow patches over a powder-blue cardigan and white button-front shirt. At times like these I wonder how his patients don't fall madly in love with him. Maybe they do, and he doesn't tell me.

Damon ordered a beer, and I asked him about his workday.

"Fine," he said, which kind of pissed me off. He always says his work day is fine, which is Damon's way of telling me what I already know: Everything that occurs in his office is confidential. I get it. Doctor-patient blah blah blah. In theory I'm all for it. God knows I don't want my therapist discussing my neuroses with his significant other over a Cobb salad. ("Next time we come here I'm going to ask for less Roquefort and more avocado. The balance is a little off. Oh, get this, Clinton Kelly is convinced that his friends and family actually hate him but are being nice to him only out of some twisted sense of obligation. Ha. What a douche.") But sometimes I would like to hear about other people's problems, if only to gauge my own level of fucked-upness. No such luck tonight.

"How was your day?" Damon asked.

"Oh, you know, the usual," I said. "Two *Chews* and some other stuff. Oh, and Paula Deen called me a turd in the punchbowl."

"Charming. How did that come about?"

I relayed the story to Damon—the fork, the wing, the sauce—and he asked me exactly what you'd expect a psychologist to ask: "And how do you feel about that?"

Sometimes I tell him not to therapize me, but not this evening. I kind of wanted my head shrunk. "I'm pretty pissed off," I said. "What kind of guest calls the host of a show a turd? So vulgar. But I also don't care, you know? Paula Deen doesn't like me. Who gives a shit? I should wear that turd like a badge of honor."

"Or like a necklace," Damon said.

Confused, I asked, "A necklace?"

"Like in *Priscilla Queen of the Desert*." And he quoted: "'What are you telling me . . . this is an ABBA turrrd?'"

We laughed loud enough to attract the attention of other

diners, most of whom smiled at us, as if they had been in on the joke. I always like when that happens; it reminds me that people actually want to see other people happy.

We finished our dinner and walked a few blocks to pick up Mary from the sitter. The sun, having set not too long ago, left a purplish stain on the sky. And save for some clanging at a nearby construction site, our neighborhood was almost as peaceful as it had been that morning. I asked Damon to hold Mary's leash so I could check my phone, which was vibrating thanks to two texts from my mother. Evidently she had just watched *The Chew* on DVR. The first text read, "Paula Deen. Rude, huh?" And the second contained two emojis: the smiling pile of poo and the yellow face baring its teeth. So my mother had indeed heard Paula Deen call me a turd. *How embarrassing is that?*

I slowed my walk down to text my mother back ("Yeah, she's pure class," plus the pig emoji) and fell about twenty steps behind Damon and Mary. When I looked up from my phone, I noticed they were crossing the street ahead of me. Technically they were jaywalking, but there was barely any traffic. Plus, the city has been in the process of replacing the Tribeca water mains for over a year, so the nearby crosswalks were closed. As Damon and Mary stepped onto the sidewalk, a car slowly making a left turn came fairly close to hitting them, which was completely unnecessary. And then I saw the driver lower his window and turn his bald head back toward Damon and Mary, as if he were about to say something nasty.

Not today, prick, I thought. *I'm not in the mood for a smart mouth.* So, I walked up to the other side of his car and gave it a good swift kick in the ass from the opposite side. Not a dainty tip-of-the-shoe tap, but a full-sole thump to his passenger-side fender (though, sadly, it wasn't enough of a thump to leave a dent). The driver, a rough-looking guy in his late thirties, stopped his car in the middle of the block and got out.

"What the fuck was that?" he yelled.

"You almost ran me over!" I yelled back. "You should really watch where you're going." Okay, it was a whitish lie. He almost ran over my husband and dog, not me. But he could have run me over. He wasn't watching where he was going because he had his head cocked out the window.

Damon and Mary stopped on the sidewalk and stared at the scene in puzzled horror. I continued walking toward them, my back to the furious driver. I glanced over my shoulder at him, wondering if he was aiming a gun in our general direction. Luckily he was not, but he did reach under his dashboard. *Maybe that's where he keeps his gun*, I thought. But then I saw his trunk pop open. I've seen enough angry white man movies to know this means "I've got a crowbar (or baseball bat) in my trunk and I'm not afraid to use it."

"Are we gonna do this?" he barked.

Do this? I thought. That doesn't make any sense. How can I "do this" without a crowbar of my own? That's like challenging a guy with no legs to a kickboxing match.

"Go fuck yourself, asshole!" I yelled and turned around. "Let's go," I said to Damon under my breath. "Now."

We were just a block away from our apartment, where we would be safe from any more confrontation. Damon looked at me as though a third nipple had just sprouted out of my forehead. "What the hell just happened?" he asked.

"I don't know," I said. "I think I have some anger issues."

"You think?"

We both laughed nervously. I took this as a good sign that

Damon wasn't considering divorcing me for being a complete lunatic. But then I realized if I were a nutjob whose car was just firmly thumped, I'd probably drive around the block to see where the two gays with the little white dog lived. So that's when I said to Damon in a low but firm voice: "Pick up the dog and run."

"What?" he said.

"Pick up the dog and run, before that guy has time to make it around the block!"

But, no, he didn't run. The man who does some form of cardio about five days a week won't move his ass faster than a leisurely stroll when I tell him to. He's on his own, I figured. I grabbed Mary's leash out of his hand, scooped her up under my arm like a football, and hightailed it down the street.

When I arrived at our front door, I saw that Damon had quickened his pace to a light trot, the way grandpa might power walk around the mall for exercise.

"Hurry up!" I yelled, holding the door open for him.

"I'm wearing loafers," he said.

When he finally made it inside, I looked around to make sure the angry driver hadn't come around the corner. "Whew, that was close," I said.

Damon seemed more amused than concerned about retaliation. "This is really not like you."

"Yeah. No shit."

I could hardly sleep again that night, not because of the dog. But because I let someone get under my skin. And because of that I acted aggressively toward someone who may or may not have deserved it. If you're the guy whose car I kicked that night, I'm sorry. I feel like the turd in the punchbowl for doing it. Please forgive me.

FREAKIN' FABULOUS, THE SITCOM

As far as I can tell there are only two activities in which I participate for no purpose other than fueling ridiculous fantasies: buying lottery tickets and writing sitcom scripts.

At any given time a half-dozen Mega Millions tickets lie crumpled at the bottom of my briefcase or gym bag, completely oblivious to the fact that they have zero chance of ever being scanned or manually checked against winning numbers in a newspaper. What's the point? I know my odds of contracting chlamydia from a Peruvian nun are greater than those of winning a hundred million dollars, and I don't care. I pay the Idiot Tax—you gotta be in it to win it!—so I can spend the following hour, sometimes more, sometimes less, thinking about all the philanthropic and completely selfish things I'd do with the money, stuff like opening a sanctuary for neglected dogs, paying for my nephews' college tuitions, buying an apartment in Paris, and, if I win the *really* big jackpot, buying Twitter just so I can unplug the fucking thing.

Creating sitcoms serves a similar purpose. I'll stay in bed for the weekend, usually only if the weather's crappy in Connecticut, scribbling away with my favorite pen in a Moleskine notebook and bringing to life silly characters loosely based on people I know. I'll imagine which actors will play the roles, what the sets should look like, which lines will get the most laughter when delivered correctly. And when I'm done, I throw the notebook in a drawer, never to be opened again.

Damon occasionally suggests that I show a script to my agent, but I can't be bothered, I say. Hollywood will just ruin everything. Some prepubescent network executive will suggest the main character, a sexually repressed, middle-aged physics professor, be played by Khloé Kardashian or insist that instead of San Francisco the show take place in Wichita because San Francisco is "where all the gays live—doesn't play well in the red states." I prefer to let these things live in my mind, where I control everything.

Here, I'm including a sitcom script about a makeover show I wrote during a sleet storm that lasted two days. We could barely step outside the house because everything was covered in a solid inch of ice. Even our dog, Mary, was getting frustrated trying to pee. In her canine urinary crouch, she'd slide down the driveway like one of those Olympic curling stones. It was hilarious. In the evening over a bottle of port, Damon and I joked that we should bring a couple of brooms outside with us and furiously sweep the ice ahead of her to see how much speed she could gain. Maybe see if she could knock down a few frozen squirrels set up like bowling pins.

Just FYI: Don't try to read between the lines for hidden digs at my *What Not to Wear* coworkers. Seriously. It's complete fiction. No, seriously.

CHARACTERS:

CHETLEY MELBOURNE, 45, hails from New Canaan, Connecticut. He's a clothing stylist with a penchant for breaking into Broadway show tunes. He's quirky, slightly snobby, mildly insecure, and impeccably dressed in an Old Hollywood style. Chetley began his career as a wardrobe intern on "Miss Saigon" and moved to Los Angeles when the show's star, Lea Salonga, was invited to sing "A Whole New World" at the Oscars. ("They sent me there to steam her gown and I never looked back!") Ever since his divorce two years ago, he's been unable to find love because, as he says, "When you're a gay single man over the age of 35 in Los Angeles, you might as well be a straight single woman over the age of 35 in Los Angeles—invisible."

SHARNAY SIMMONS, 42, is originally from Toronto, where she attended a prestigious all-girls boarding school. At the age of 16 she was arrested for using a fake ID to enter a club during a weekend outing in New York City. On the bright side, a model scout had also been arrested that night for cocaine possession. The result was a lucrative and lengthy modeling career for Sharnay, which allowed her to travel the world, fine-tune her sense of style, and eventually become a fashion stylist on "You Look Fabulous."

MINNIE MAI, 21, is a half-Chinese, half-Jewish makeup artist from Minneapolis. When her parents would not let her skip college to pursue a Hollywood makeup career, she doubled up on classes at Northwestern University and finished her bachelor's degree in chemistry in two years. While in school she created a popular blog called "Mai Face" in which she tested every cosmetic known to womankind. It quickly became rated as the best beauty blog by many major women's magazines. Minnie is energetic, smart (though a little immature), media-savvy, and always clad in the latest trends.

JUAN CARLOS RODRIGUEZ, 33, is a modern-day Warren Beatty in "Shampoo." He's Puerto Rican-American, very charming, and very attractive. His hairstyling career began in his mother's shop in the South Bronx, where she put him to work at the age of 12 to keep him out of trouble. He eventually worked his way up to styling hair in Manhattan's most exclusive salons and writing a very popular blog called "Whoomp, Hair It Is." Juan Carlos is very aware of his good looks and is an equal-opportunity flirt, causing others to frequently question his sexuality.

FIONA WHITTINGCOMB, 39, is the executive producer of "You Look Fabulous." Originally from London, Fiona is the queen of makeover television, having produced several shows in the genre for the BBC. Fiona comes off as superior and judgmental, not just because she's British, but because she's also a bitch.

ACT ONE

FADE IN:

Montage of clips from "You Look Fabulous"—a flashy makeover show.

CHETLEY (V.O.) *Hi. My name is Chetley Melbourne, the guy from "You Look Fabulous." I know, I know, you love that show. And why shouldn't you. It's the most successful makeover series in the history of television. "You Look Fabulous" stars me—that's Chetley Melbourne if you weren't paying attention—and Sharnay Simmons, as well as [BLEEP] and [BLEEP]. Well, it doesn't star [BLEEP] and [BLEEP] anymore. Those two got fired, just earlier today as a matter of fact, and evidently things got a little ugly.*

Security cam footage of one woman, face blurred, throwing punches wildly at guards, and a man, face blurred, on his hands and knees begging and sobbing.

CHETLEY (V.O.) (CONT'D) *Sharnay and I did not get fired, although I wouldn't have minded too much. She and I have been hosting this show for nine years. That's a long time to be saying the same crap, over and over and over.*

Repetitive clips of Sharnay and Chetley exclaiming "You look fabulous!" to women who have been made over.

CHETLEY (V.O.) (CONT'D) *I guess I shouldn't complain about my job. It pays the mortgage . . . on my mansion!*

Shot of Chetley having a martini on a lounge chair in the backyard of a huge house. A handsome, shirtless pool boy is working nearby. Chetley winks to camera.

CHETLEY (V.O.) (CONT'D) *But enough about me, at least for now. Let's talk about Sharnay. Isn't she pretty? A real natural beauty—if it's natural to employ three hairstylists, two makeup artists, four wardrobe stylists, and one guy whose sole job it is to apply her liquid eyeliner.*

Montage of assistants holding up dresses, jewelry, shoes, and wigs for Sharnay's approval.

CHETLEY (V.O.) (CONT'D) *In all these years, I've only seen her without makeup once. I literally mistook her for the home-health aide who takes care of my 92-year-old grandfather.*

INT. HALLWAY – DAY CUT TO: Sharnay is walking in a bathrobe, hair in a sloppy bun, with her back to camera. CHETLEY comes from around the corner and mistakes her for someone else.

CHETLEY (CONT'D) (startled and worried) Oh my God, what are you doing here? Is something wrong with Pop-Pop?!? (realizes who she actually is, then awkwardly tries to cover) Oh . . . I mean, Hey! What's up! Pop pop! Pip pip! See you later, yo!

                    INT. FIONA'S OFFICE - DAY

CHETLEY (V.O.) *Yeah, I know. Not my best recovery, but I was scared! Anyway, we were called into Fiona's office. She's the producer of the show, as well as a complete and total B. You might assume that a soulless, backstabbing network executive and someone who has worked on a makeover series for almost a decade would have better fashion sense. But you'd be wrong.*

                          CUT TO:

FIONA sits on her desk, flipping through some paperwork. She wears thigh-high black boots, skintight black leggings, and a very poufy, high-necked white blouse.

CHETLEY (V.O.) (CONT'D) *Do you see this? Evidently today she's taking her style inspiration from Keira Knightley. In "Pirates of the Caribbean." I can't even.*

FIONA I know the two of you became very close friends of [BLEEP] and [BLEEP] over the years. Well, I've got some exciting news. They've been fired. And I've already received word that they're suing the network. So, for all intents and purposes, we're going to consider them dead. (smiles)

Sharnay and Chetley stare at each other blankly.

SHARNAY I want [BLEEP]'s parking space.

CHETLEY I want [BLEEP]'s dressing room.

SHARNAY I wanted [BLEEP]'s dressing room!

CHETLEY Well, I wanted [BLEEP]'s parking spot. Trade? Deal.

FIONA Your compassion is heartwarming.

CHETLEY (sings in an Ethel Merman voice) There's no business like show business! (suddenly concerned) (MORE)

CHETLEY (CONT'D) Are you replacing them? Season ten starts shooting today.

FIONA Of course. We've hired two new hosts.

SHARNAY Who?

FIONA I was just about to tell you. The two of you will continue to handle clothes, accessories, and shoes. The new hairstylist is named Juan Carlos Rodriguez and the new makeup artist is Minnie Mai.

SHARNAY I've never heard of them.

FIONA That's because they're new to television. They both write very popular blogs and have huge social media followings.

CHETLEY Bloggers? Is that what it's come to?

SHARNAY Who reads blogs? I've never looked at a blog in my life! What kind of word is blog anyway. Blah-g. Blah-g. Blah-g. Sounds like the ladies' room at the Beverly Hilton after lunch. (mimics vomiting) Blah-g.

CHETLEY I like the food there.

SHARNAY It's not the food, it's the clientele. (sticks finger in her mouth)

CHETLEY Oh, a bulimia joke. That's always in good taste.

Sharnay sticks out her tongue at Chetley. Chetley thumbs his nose back.

FIONA When are you two going to grow up? The network has decided to cast bloggers to attract millennials.

CHETLEY Why on earth would they do that?

FIONA Because you're not getting any younger.

Chetley gasps in horror.

SHARNAY Ha-ha.

FIONA I was referring to you also, Sharnay.

Sharnay gasps in horror.

CHETLEY Ha-ha.

FIONA (dryly) Ha-ha. I'm loath to admit that the two of you are safe, at least for the time being. Turns out you're very much loved by women 18 to 35. For the life of me I can't figure out why, but apparently my opinion doesn't matter. Unbeknownst to you, we spent a fortune on extensive market research at the end of last season, conducting focus groups in twelve major cities across America. Sharnay, young women see you as (reads limply from a bound report and uses air quotes) "glamorous," "inspiring," and "a good role model." (rolls eyes) And Chetley, women in the demo see you as "a best friend," "a favorite gay uncle," and "the kind of guy you want to have a cosmo with."

CHETLEY A cosmo? That's so 2003. Who the hell do I look like, Cynthia Nixon?

SHARNAY No, she's much more butch than you nowadays.

Sharnay and Chetley mouth the word "lesbian" to each other.

FIONA (annoyed) I think it's time for you to meet your new cohosts. They're waiting in the conference room next door. (speaks into intercom) Diane, please send in Juan Carlos and Minnie. (to Sharnay and Chetley) Did I mention they're much younger than you?

MINNIE enters.

MINNIE Juan Carlos said he'd be right in. I think he's making a pee-pee. What's up, bitches! I'm Minnie Mai! Not to be confused with Mini Me! It is so freakin' amaze-balls to meet you guys! I have been watching this show since I was—I don't know—twelve. You know, right around puberty, when the boobies really started growing, or not growing in my case. Ha-ha! These are totes fakes. I got C-cups because I didn't want to look all "Me so horny." You know what I mean? Me love you long time. I should really S.T.F.U., but I can't help it. When I get nervous I turn into a racial stereotype. (to Sharnay) O.M.G.! Your hair is gorge! Can I touch? (she touches without waiting for an answer) That's nice. Silky. Not Chinese because it takes a curl nicely. Probably Indian. Could also be Cambodian hooker.

Sharnay looks stunned and furious. Chetley is amused.

DIANE (ON INTERCOM) Juan Carlos is back. I'm sending him in now.

FIONA Thank you. Let's stop with the touching. I'm sufficiently repulsed.

JUAN CARLOS enters.

Sharnay and Chetley both gasp in surprise. They look at each other with suspicion and quickly cover.

Fiona and Minnie look at each other and shrug. Juan Carlos smiles.

CUT TO BLACK.

END OF ACT ONE.

ACT TWO INT. FIONA'S OFFICE - DAY

Chetley, Sharnay, Minnie, and Juan Carlos are seated in Fiona's office. She is handing out packets of photographs and biographical infor-mation, which the hosts peruse.

CHETLEY (V.O.) *Let's return to our meeting, shall we? Fun.*

FIONA Today you're making over a woman named Angie Grober. The field team shot her at-home story last week. Mom of nine. Five or six of them are adopted. Cancer survivor. Blah, blah, blah. It's all in the packet. As you can see from her pictures, she's tragic. She's not too fat though, and she has decent bone structure.

JUAN CARLOS Not too fat? It says here she's a size six.

FIONA Like I said, not "too" fat.

SHARNAY Does she have all her—

FIONA (interrupting) Yes, Sharnay, she has all her teeth. You don't have to ask me that every week.

SHARNAY (confrontational) I'm asking because I don't want a repeat of season four, when every woman you cast was missing a big-ole toof in the front of her mouth. (to Minnie and Juan Carlos) You can put a girl in an Armani gown, pile ten pounds of extensions on her head, and give her a to-die-for smoky eye. But if she smiles and half her grille is back in Kentucky, all your hard work is for nothing.

CHETLEY Amen, sister.

MINNIE We could always get them veneers.

FIONA This show doesn't do cosmetic procedures. No cutting, drilling, injecting. Not even Botox. The guiding principle of this show is helping a woman's inner beauty shine outward.

SHARNAY (sarcastic) As long as she's not too ugly to begin with. Right, Fiona?

FIONA Correct. Juan Carlos, do you have any ideas what you'd like to do with her hair?

JUAN CARLOS I was thinking she might look good as a buttery blonde, with some extra highlights around the face and maybe bangs . . .

CHETLEY (V.O.) *I thought that meeting would never end. Now I can tell you why Sharnay and I gasped when Juan Carlos entered the office.*

DISSOLVE TO: INT. LADIES' ROOM - DAY Sharnay has been frantically looking for Chetley. She finds him in the ladies' room.

SHARNAY I have been looking all over for you! What are you doing in the ladies' room?

CHETLEY I was looking for you! Then I got distracted by the fact that there's potpourri in here. We don't have potpourri in the men's room. And I cannot for the life of me figure out what that smell is. (holds bowl up to her nose) Is that peach?

SHARNAY Get that [BLEEP] out of my face. I need you to spill the beans right now!

CHETLEY I don't have any beans.

SHARNAY You are full of beans! I saw the way you acted when the new guy showed up.

CHETLEY I saw the way *you* acted when the new guy showed up.

SHARNAY I don't know what you're talking about.

CHETLEY I don't know what *you're* talking about.

SHARNAY Stop repeating everything I say or I am gonna get all Bed-Stuy on your ass.

CHETLEY Bed-Stuy? As in Bedford Stuyvesant? Brooklyn?

SHARNAY Yeah, what about it?

CHETLEY Oh, please. You're from Toronto. You went to prep school.

SHARNAY (whining) OK, OK. Just tell me. I need to know what's up with you and him.

CHETLEY Fine. I don't need this to become common knowledge around here, but I'm 99 percent sure I . . . you know . . . fooled around with him.

SHARNAY Shut. Your. Face!

CHETLEY It was two years ago, after I got gay divorced.

SHARNAY I don't believe you.

CHETLEY Why not? You don't believe a guy like me could score a hottie like him?

SHARNAY I'm sure you could. On a good day.

CHETLEY Or is it because you don't believe he's gay, because let me tell you . . . (sassy) He ain't that butch.

SHARNAY Don't do the black girl thing with your neck. I've told you, it's not cute when you do it. It's cute when I do it. That's not what I meant.

CHETLEY What's your problem then?

SHARNAY I think I fooled around with him too.

CHETLEY Liar!

SHARNAY I am not!

CHETLEY You are just saying that to copy me!

SHARNAY Wrong!

CHETLEY It's just like that time last season when I told Fiona I wanted wheatgrass-and-aloe juice for lunch every day. And then you said, "Yes, Fiona, I'll have that too!"

SHARNAY We were doing the same juice cleanse, remember? It was your idea.

CHETLEY Oh, right.

SHARNAY You kept the weight off.

CHETLEY Aww, thank you for noticing.

SHARNAY Look, I'm not yanking your chain. I'm serious. It was the only one-night stand of my life!

CHETLEY Right. And I'm Cynthia Nixon. (laughs) Like the way I brought her up twice in one day? What are the chances?

SHARNAY Shush. I'm not kidding. I don't usually put out so easily. I'm no prude, don't get me wrong, but I always wait till the third date. Then I will hit it. And I will hit. It. Hard! You know what I'm talkin' about?

CHETLEY Please, I'm already nauseous from the potpourri. What happened this time?

SHARNAY I was in Cabo two winters ago with my friend Sandra. We were having umbrella drinks and she ended up not feeling so well. She had too much sun or something, so she went back to our hotel room. But I stayed and had one more.

Shot of Sharnay sitting alone at a slightly tacky hotel bar. She is approached by a tall stranger whose face we cannot see.

SHARNAY (CONT'D) Then this mysterious, super-cute guy shows up and asks me to dance. Well, one thing led to another and the next thing I know I'm sneaking out of his room at three a.m.

Shot of Sharnay, disheveled and shoes in hand, closing a hotel room door behind her.

SHARNAY (CONT'D) Sandra and I left the next morning, so I never saw him again.

CHETLEY He never told you his name?

SHARNAY I didn't ask.

CHETLEY I don't understand why you can't be sure it's Juan Carlos.

SHARNAY He had a mustache!

CHETLEY A disguise!

SHARNAY I don't understand why *you* can't be sure.

CHETLEY He told me his name was Hector.

SHARNAY An alias!

CHETLEY Mango!

SHARNAY What?

CHETLEY The potpourri is mango.

SHARNAY You're a freak.

                    INT. CHANGING ROOM SET - DAY

CUT TO: Sharnay and Chetley are helping their makeover subject, Angie, find the perfect dress. There are racks of clothes all around the room. Angie remains behind a swinging door.

CHETLEY (V.O.) *Later that day, despite our burning curiosity, we had to get to work on our makeover.*

SHARNAY (throws a dress over the top of changing room door) Here, Angie, try this dress. We'll find one that works. Don't worry. (looks at Chetley and crosses her fingers

Minnie enters.

MINNIE Hey, you guys have a minute?

CHETLEY Sure. What's up?

MINNIE I feel like we got off on the wrong foot this morning. It's just that I'm a huge fan and I'm so excited to be working with you. Can we be friends? Please?

SHARNAY Of course. Just don't touch my hair again, girl.

CHETLEY That [BLEEP] don't like to be touched.

MINNIE Why is it that every time I see the two of you, you're whispering and telling secrets? I'm starting to get a complex.

SHARNAY We're not whispering about you.

CHETLEY We're whispering about Juan Carlos.

MINNIE Total stud, right?

SHARNAY Did you know him before you got this show?

ANGIE (peeks head over changing room door) It's too tight!

CHETLEY How tight? Like, I-need-Spanx tight or I-need-a-crowbar tight?

ANGIE I don't know.

CHETLEY (rolls eyes) Let me see. (peeks in changing room) OK, so it's a little too tight. (makes a face to Sharnay to say it's terrible) We'll go one size up.

Sharnay holds up one finger to question "one size up." Chetley holds up three fingers to indicate three sizes up.

SHARNAY (to Minnie) So, did you know him?

MINNIE No, this morning was the first time I met him.

CHETLEY Do you know if he likes boys?

SHARNAY Or girls?

CHETLEY Or both? (throws another dress over the changing room door) Here's another one.

MINNIE Oh, I get it. You both have crushes on him. How cute. And a little sad.

SHARNAY That's not it. (whispers) We think we may have hooked up with him.

MINNIE (horrified) At the same time?

CHETLEY Gross.

SHARNAY No!

MINNIE I don't understand. What do you mean, you "think" you hooked up with him? Why doesn't someone "know" that kind of thing?

SHARNAY He had a mustache when he was with me.

CHETLEY And he told me his name was Hector!

MINNIE Ohhhh . . . sneaky.

SHARNAY Shhh.

Fiona and Juan Carlos enter.

FIONA Is Angie ready for hair and makeup? We're almost behind schedule.

CHETLEY Almost behind schedule? What does that even mean? Either you're behind schedule or you're not. That's like saying you *almost* won the lottery. Or you *almost* touched the back of George Stephanopoulos' neck while he was asleep next to you on the red-eye. But you didn't because that would be creepy and maybe even illegal.

SHARNAY She'll be ready in time, Fiona.

ANGIE I think this one looks good!

SHARNAY Let's see.

Angie steps out of changing room in a voluminous silver gown.

SHARNAY (CONT'D) It's OK. Not perfect. Let's try something else.

Angie, dejected, returns to changing room.

FIONA That dress was lovely. If you have a fetish for stove-top popcorn. Look, I don't need to remind the two of you that if we go over schedule, we run into tens of thousands of dollars in overtime charges with the crew. I will not tolerate that at all this season.

(MORE)

FIONA (CONT'D) Juan Carlos, hair is up next so, let's make sure your station is to your liking.

MINNIE Aw, don't go yet!

FIONA Why not?

MINNIE (scrambling) Juan Carlos has something on his face. I wouldn't want him to go on TV with an eye booger or anything.

FIONA I don't see anything.

MINNIE (to Juan Carlos) Come here. Shut your eyes.

Minnie points Juan Carlos' face toward Sharnay. She takes a piece of her own hair and creates a mustache on Juan Carlos' face with it. She looks at Sharnay as if to ask if that rings any bells. Sharnay is still unsure.

FIONA Come on, Juan Carlos. Minnie, I suggest you get your makeup station set up. We shoot makeup after hair.

MINNIE It's all set up.

Fiona and Juan Carlos begin to leave.

MINNIE (CONT'D) Wait! I feel like we all hardly know each other.

FIONA (tugging at Juan Carlos) There will be plenty of time to get to know each other in the future. (dryly) Believe me.

MINNIE Let's play a game!

FIONA A what?

MINNIE A game. The name game! I say a letter and you have to say the first name that pops into your head. It's hilarious. (points to Chetley) Your letter is "L." Go!

CHETLEY Larry.

MINNIE Yes! (points to Sharnay) "F." Go!

SHARNAY Frank!

MINNIE Great! (points to Juan Carlos) "H." Go!

JUAN CARLOS Hector.

MINNIE Aha! Hector! That's a good one!

FIONA Enough! This is a serious television show, Miss Mai, not the inane blog you write. I suggest you start behaving more professionally or your first episode of "You Look Fabulous" will be your last.

Fiona and Juan Carlos exit.

ANGIE (peeking out over top of door) Oooh, you in trouble, girl.

CUT TO BLACK.

END OF ACT TWO.

ACT THREE

INT. CHANGING ROOM SET - CONTINUOUS

SHARNAY Don't let Fiona bother you.

CHETLEY She's really charming once you get to know her.

Sharnay and Minnie give skeptical looks.

CHETLEY (CONT'D) I'm totally lying. She's a demon.

MINNIE Who does she think she is, calling me by my last name. Miss Mai. Miss Mai ass, skank. My real last name is Lefkowitz anyway. My father's Jewish.

CHETLEY Get out! I'm a half-breed too. Half WASP, half Jewish. Jewish mother though. So technically, I'm more Jewish than you. Except I never had a bar mitzvah, so technically I'm not Jewish. I think. I told my parents that for my thirteenth birthday, instead of a bar mitzvah I wanted a private performance of "A Chorus Line" in our backyard. My parents were crazy-rich, so they basically bought me Donna McKechnie.

MINNIE I don't know who that is, but mazel.

ANGIE (exiting changing room in a boldly printed caftan) This is the twenty-third dress I've tried on and nothing looks good.

SHARNAY Oh, stop. It looks good. If you're hosting a key party.

CHETLEY Or if you're married to Mister Roper. "Stanley, would you stop bothering those kids upstairs!"

MINNIE I don't know who that is either.

CHETLEY You really need to brush up on your 1970s pop culture.

MINNIE I was born in 1992.

CHETLEY Sharnay, she was born—in the '90s.

SHARNAY (to Chetley) I'm not deaf. (to Angie) You still haven't tried on the orange satin sheath.

CHETLEY (to Angie) It's gonna be fabulous! Back inside. And hurry!

Angie returns to changing room.

CHETLEY (CONT'D) 1992. I got my start in this business in 1992. It's true. I was Christina Applegate's stylist in "Married . . . With Children." Fishnet tights with denim shorts? That was me. You're welcome.

SHARNAY So, where were we? We know Juan Carlos is really Hector. (to Minnie) You're a genius, by the way. But we still don't know for sure if I slept with him.

MINNIE We'll need to figure out another way to trick him. When were you with him?

SHARNAY Two years ago.

MINNIE Where?

SHARNAY Cabo San Lucas.

MINNIE I'm on it!

Minnie leaves.

Angie opens up dressing room door. She wears the orange dress and it fits perfectly.

ANGIE How's this?

CHETLEY Ladies and gentlemen, we have a winner!

SHARNAY Yay! Orange you glad you tried that one on?

Chetley and Angie groan.

INT. HAIR AND MAKEUP SET - DAY CUT TO: *Juan Carlos straightens up his hairstyling station. Fiona rifles through Minnie's makeup station.*

FIONA I see Minnie has set up her station after all. Quite an assortment.

(starts applying lipstick)

JUAN CARLOS You probably shouldn't be doing that.

FIONA You probably shouldn't be telling me what to do.

Minnie enters.

JUAN CARLOS You probably want to know that Minnie is right behind you.

MINNIE Hi!

FIONA I was just admiring your makeup assortment.

MINNIE That's a pretty shade you chose. It's called "Scarlet Fever." Which is interesting because I used it just yesterday on a drag queen with really bad herpes.

FIONA (wiping mouth) Yuck.

MINNIE Oh, don't worry. I always use disposable brushes. I'm kind of a cleanliness freak. (she wipes the top layer of lipstick off the tube) That's why I don't like anyone touching my things without asking.

FIONA I had high hopes for you, Miss Mai. Now I'm starting to question the network's decision to hire you.

MINNIE I'm sorry to hear that but I assure you I'm a professional. And thank you for understanding about not using my supplies. (hesitates for a second) Especially not the brow gel.

FIONA The brow gel?

MINNIE This stuff. (picks up small tube) It's very expensive. I have it shipped from Japan. I can only get one tube at a time through customs.

FIONA What's so special about it?

MINNIE Well, it's really easy to apply. And it makes for perfect eyebrows every time. And I always keep it right here. (puts tube down very deliberately)

FIONA Good to know. I'm going to check up on Sharnay and Chetley. How long does it take to find one stupid dress?

Fiona exits.

MINNIE That chick hates me.

JUAN CARLOS Like a Puerto Rican hates birth control. (pause) I'm Puerto Rican. I can say those things. What's up?

MINNIE Not much. I was just thinking about my next vacation.

JUAN CARLOS Interesting thing to do on your first day of work.

MINNIE Never too early to start planning for a good time, I always say. Where do you think I should go?

JUAN CARLOS What kind of vacation do you want?

MINNIE A sexy beach vacation.

JUAN CARLOS You could go to Thailand.

MINNIE Too far.

JUAN CARLOS There's always Mexico.

MINNIE Yes, Mexico! Do you have a favorite part?

JUAN CARLOS I always have a good time in Cabo.

MINNIE I knew it! Cabo!

JUAN CARLOS I just realized I left my favorite hair dryer in the car. I'll catch you later.

INT. CHANGING ROOM SET - LATER THAT DAY CUT TO: *Sharnay and Chetley are sitting on the floor. Only Angie's legs and feet are visible. She is trying, with little success, to walk in a pair of five-inch platform stilettos.*

CHETLEY C'mon, Angie, you can do this!

ANGIE I can't.

CHETLEY These heels are nothing! I styled someone in these exact shoes just last week. It was Ruth Ginsberg. She was doing a charity walkathon.

SHARNAY Try, Angie. Shoulders back, boobs out. (to Chetley quietly) This is more painful than watching a brain-damaged giraffe take its first steps.

Minnie enters. Sits on floor.

MINNIE (to Sharnay) He told me he always has fun in Cabo. You totally had sex with him! (to Chetley) And so did you! You know that saying: When you have sex with someone it's like you're having sex with everyone they've ever had sex with? Well, if that's true, you two have totally done it with each other.

CHETLEY Please don't tell me that. For the record, I just fooled around with him. A little bit of "eh." And a little bit of "eh." Not the full "eh-eh."

SHARNAY I did the full "eh-eh."

MINNIE Man, I hate that he's being so coy!

SHARNAY Me too!

CHETLEY Me three!

Angie falls flat on her face in front of them.

INT. HAIR AND MAKEUP SET - CONTINUOUS

Fiona rifles through Minnie's makeup station again.

CHETLEY (V.O.) *Meanwhile, someone had a case of the sticky fingers.*

FIONA Hell if I'll let that little brat tell me what I can and can't touch. (applies brow gel to both of her eyebrows)

INT. HAIR AND MAKEUP SET - LATER THAT DAY *Juan Carlos is finishing up a haircut.* CUT TO:

CHETLEY (V.O.) *And later, Juan Carlos proved to be an excellent hairstylist—and television host.*

JUAN CARLOS Angie, I am all done with you. I think your hair looks gorgeous, but I can't let you see yourself yet. It's a surprise! Next up, makeup.

FLOOR MANAGER Cut! Nice work, Juan Carlos.

JUAN CARLOS Thank you.

FLOOR MANAGER Angie, please take a seat in the makeup chair. Minnie, we'd love to start immediately with you if you're ready.

MINNIE Ready, Freddie.

FLOOR MANAGER That's what I like. Coming to you in 3 . . . 2 . . . 1 . . .

MINNIE Hi, Angie, my name is Minnie and I'll be doing your makeup today. I'd really love to bring out those beautiful green eyes of yours . . .

INT. BACKSTAGE - CONTINUOUS FADE TO: *Fiona is watching the action on set. She scratches her brow and notices a single eyebrow hair on her fingers. She blows it off. She touches her brow again and this time two hairs come off in her hand. She runs to a mirror nearby and rubs a section of her right eyebrow and it completely falls off. She muffles her own scream and is hushed by the Floor Manager.*

CUT TO: INT. BACKSTAGE - NEARBY - CONTINUOUS *Sharnay and Chetley stand side by side. They are also watching Minnie on set. They notice Fiona's commotion and ignore it.*

SHARNAY (about Minnie) She's good.

CHETLEY Very natural.

Juan Carlos sneaks up behind them and whispers in their ears.

JUAN CARLOS Hey, sexy.

CHETLEY (suspicious) Which one of us are you talking to?

JUAN CARLOS Both of you.

SHARNAY Can we help you?

JUAN CARLOS I know what you two are up to.

SHARNAY Is that so?

JUAN CARLOS You're trying to figure out which of you has made sweet love to me.

CHETLEY We've already figured it out. And we're already over it. It's both of us.

JUAN CARLOS Incorrect. It's only one of you.

SHARNAY (shocked) Which one?

JUAN CARLOS I'll tell you later.

He exits. Sharnay and Chetley stare at each other in disbelief. CUT TO:

INT. TELEVISION STUDIO - MOMENTS LATER Chetley, Sharnay, Minnie, and Juan Carlos stand in a row on the main set of "You Look Fabulous." They are preparing for the last shot of the day, the final reveal.

FLOOR MANAGER Thank you for your patience, guys. We'll be ready to roll in less than two minutes.

FIONA (O.C.) Minnie! Come here!

MINNIE What?

She runs off set. The others don't know what's wrong.

CUT TO: INT. BACKSTAGE - CONTINUOUS

FIONA (holding her hand over her forehead) What did you put in that brow gel?

MINNIE Nothing. Why?

FIONA You know why.

MINNIE I asked you not to touch it.

FIONA What was in it?

MINNIE It's a depilatory. It's for people who don't like plucking. You apply the gel to unwanted hairs and they just fall right out.

FIONA I thought it was for taming brows, like all brow gels.

MINNIE Not this stuff. Don't tell me you . . .

INT. TELEVISION STUDIO - DAY CUT TO: *Sharnay, Chetley, and Juan Carlos are still on set waiting for the action cue.*

FLOOR MANAGER Minnie! We need you on set now!

Minnie runs in and takes her place.

MINNIE Well, it was nice working with you guys.

SHARNAY What happened?

MINNIE I'm sure you'll find out soon enough.

JUAN CARLOS It was . . . Sharnay.

SHARNAY (stifled excitement) I knew it! (speaking out the side of her mouth to Juan Carlos) It was good, right?

JUAN CARLOS Excellent.

CHETLEY I'm confused.

MINNIE Me too. Who is Hector?

JUAN CARLOS My twin brother.

MINNIE Yeah, right.

JUAN CARLOS I'm serious. (takes out phone and begins to scroll through photos) Look, I have a million pictures of him and me. Here we are in matching sailor suits as a kid. Here we are with mustaches. He's a gay.

MINNIE Cute.

JUAN CARLOS Sorry, Chet. I remembered that about two years ago he told me he fooled around with some guy from a TV show. I figured it must be you.

CHETLEY Great. I'm just some guy from a TV show.

JUAN CARLOS He also told me you— (whispers in Chetley's ear)

CHETLEY Well, that makes me feel a little better.

MINNIE I'm glad we figured this all out, ya big bunch of hose-bags.

FLOOR MANAGER We're coming to you, Sharnay, in 3 . . . 2 . . . 1 . . .

SHARNAY OK, Angie, it's time to come out!

CHETLEY Show us your new look!

Angie comes out from behind a curtain. She looks happy and beautiful, with her orange dress, moderate heels, sassy haircut, and perfect makeup. The camera pans to Fiona who scowls—without eyebrows.

CHETLEY, SHARNAY, MINNIE, AND JUAN CARLOS You look fabulous!

CUT TO BLACK.

END OF ACT THREE.

ACT FOUR (TAG)

Fiona sits, back to camera. Minnie is repairing Fiona's eyebrows.

FIONA I'm sorry I used your products without permission.

MINNIE I forgive you. I'm sorry your eyebrows fell out.

FIONA Nice work on Angie today.

MINNIE Thank you. So I'm not fired?

FIONA No. Not yet.

MINNIE OK, I'm done drawing them back on. I think they look very natural.

Fiona picks up a hand-mirror. Minnie has drawn on exaggerated Joan Crawford-style brows.

FIONA Minnie!

MINNIE No more wire hangers!

FIONA Not funny!

MINNIE It was a joke! I'll do them right this time!

CUT TO BLACK.

So, there you have it. One of my many ideas that will never come to fruition, and I'm OK with that. As I mentioned, I prefer these characters live in my head than on a television screen anyway. My head's nice and safe. And most important of all, I'm in control of it. At least I think I am. Anyway, gotta run. PowerBall is up to 300 million bucks and I am gonna *win* it this time! That is, if I ever scan the damn ticket.

THE SWITCH

The second time I met Damon was the first time I felt the switch, one of those moments when someone, or perhaps something, bigger, in the cosmic sense, pulls a little lever and—*click*—the track you've been traveling on is no longer your track. The old track just disappears behind you, as irrelevant as yesterday's train schedule. *Click*. You're going somewhere else now. *Click*. There's no reverse. *Click*. Your reality will never be the same.

This switch was different from all the previous switches in my life because I didn't see it coming (maybe I could have, but I'm thankful not to have), and to this day I don't know who or what flipped it, not that it matters much.

Talking to people about switches, I've learned we all have them but most of us can't pinpoint the exact moment they occur. That's because, I believe, when you see a switch in the distance, you can emotionally prepare for it; the adjustment, sometimes subtle, sometimes not, is cushioned by the emotions you've spread out before you as you chug steadily, relentlessly, toward it. Let me give you an example: When I was a child, my biological parents, who at one point—I assume—were enough in love to marry and create a family, "grew apart," and in the process failed to keep secret their utter contempt for each other. I knew on some level their union would not last, but I was consumed, naturally, with sadness and fear. They divorced, and soon I was the new kid in a new school.

My track had changed. My parents changed it, obviously, but *when*? I can't pinpoint the precise moment—and the moment *had* to be precise because one person can't ride on two tracks simultaneously. At one point, I was a ten-year-old boy in a two-parent family. At another point, I was not. The switch occurred, but I missed it. Perhaps if I had been a little older, more attuned, less sad, less frightened, I would have felt it. But I didn't. I had felt no switch, but I knew I was headed in a different direction.

That's the way life happens. Most of the time.

"Does anyone really *want* to be at this party?" I wondered while chewing a cube of vaguely Swiss cheese and watching a dozen or so female editors and reporters mill around the *What Not to Wear* studio. The series producer, a British woman named Sarah Jane, was urging two of them to step into "the dreaded three-hundred-and-sixty-degree mirror," one of the show's signature gimmicks, so they could see themselves from all angles. "I've been in once," she said. "I thought I might *die*." The event had been arranged by the publicity department to announce that the show had been picked up for another season. Good news for the cast and crew, of course, but I didn't really see the point. Why throw a half-assed party when a half-assed press release would suffice?

Fully aware that I was expected to mix and mingle, I made my way toward a trio of women in their mid- to late twenties, all of whom were wearing dark-wash boot-cut jeans, a wardrobe staple of the time.

"Hi, I'm Clinton," I said. They worked at a popular weekly entertainment magazine, according to their name tags.

"So . . . did we pass?" the most polished and outgoing of them asked, while the other two smiled halfheartedly. The question annoyed me then, as it does now, at least when used as a conversation starter. Call me old-fashioned, but I prefer when someone introduces herself with a "Hello" or a "Nice to meet you." Most of all, I enjoy an "*Enchanté*," uttered with a languidly extended gloved hand, however hard they are to come by these days.

Everywhere I went since the show became a hit, strangers in the supermarket, on the subway, in the airport would say things like *Oh my God, you're that guy from that show! How do I look? Is this what not to wear? Get it? "What not to wear"? My mother told me I'm too fat for this dress. I think she's a total bitch. What do you think?* I quickly learned it's easier to give people the attention they crave than explain to them that the peanut butter I'm buying, or the book I'm reading, or the flight I'm running to catch is more important to me *at that particular moment in time* than pointing out to a complete stranger that her ill-fitting, too-small bra is creating four bumps where there should be two and her squared-off shoes make her look like she's got club feet.

This was a professional event, however, so I turned on the charm. "Let me *see* . . . ," I said in my most affected voice and scanned the three of them from head to toe. I have created a particular facial expression for this kind of situation that conveys a winning combination of gentle playfulness, thoughtful concern, and mild disgust. "You've all passed. But I have a few . . . how do I say . . . concerns."

"Well, let's hear them," said the leader.

I started with the plainest girl in a red jersey top. She had straight brown hair and wore no accessories. She seemed the least happy to be there, as well as the least happy to be alive in general. "So . . . your blouse is bringing out some of the imperfections in your skin. It looks like you have a little rosacea."

"I do. A little," she answered quietly, her jaw clenching.

"It's no big deal. I have it too," I said. "Don't bleach your pillowcases and make sure your detergent is unscented! But anyway, I think you'll look better in cooler colors like blue or green. Oh my God! Do you know what you should try?" Almost imperceptibly she shook her head. "Purple! You should try purple! See, you have really pretty green eyes. A lot of people don't know this, but purple brings out green! Get yourself a purple blouse—like a deep aubergine—and I *guarantee* people will compliment your eyes. All. Day. Long."

She seemed to perk up a smidge at the idea. "I never thought of that," she said.

"That's why I'm here! Now, let's move on to *you*." The next girl was the heaviest of the bunch, probably a 14, which is not obese by any stretch but a solid five sizes larger than the average female magazine editor working in New York City. "I feel like your proportions are just slightly off."

"I don't know what that means," she said.

"I'll explain. See how your tunic is coming down past your tush? That makes your torso look longer than your legs. You've got great legs! Let's show them off a bit. Look for tops that hit at mid-hip. That will keep the leg line long, making you look taller and leaner."

"Thank you," she said. The sound of my own voice was making me ill. While everything I was saying was technically true, it still felt like complete bullshit.

"And now *you* . . ." I turned to the one who had asked my opinion in the first place. She stood with her right hand on her hip and her right knee slightly bent in a perfect, and most probably rehearsed, local-beauty-pageant bevel. Her closed-mouth smile told me she was confident that her outfit—expertly distressed jeans, a simple white V-neck blouse, a cropped tweed jacket with metallic threading, and snakeskin pumps—was flawless. And it was. Everything about her looked expensive, right down to her dyed-blond roots. But for some reason, I just could not tell her so. Perhaps it was because she had asked for my opinion knowing full well that she was dressed better than her colleagues. Had she only asked, "Did *I* pass?" I would have said, "With straight As, girl!" But she didn't. She had used the word *we* and implicated two, possibly innocent, bystanders. I toyed with the idea of telling her she looked like she was trying too hard, but that would have been a lie. She looked effortlessly chic, the bitch.

Then I noticed the mole.

She had one of those puffy, three-dimensional moles—the kind that nice girls from good families with overbearing mothers have removed by a dermatologist—on her décolletage. And the diamond (real or fake, I couldn't tell) pendant shaped like an asymmetrical heart dangling from the baby chain around her neck was stuck to it, off-kilter, when it should have been hanging straight down. I felt simultaneously relieved and saddened. The former because she was not as perfect as she projected, and I was perceptive enough to realize it. The latter because I was certain this mole was standing between her and true love. I could imagine a man saying to her, innocuously but perhaps recklessly,

"Why don't you get that taken care of?," which she would find either controlling or shallow. And so she would break up with him, despite the fact that he was otherwise quite caring and maybe just a bit mole-phobic. It's a little fucked up, but that's the way my mind works. Sometimes dumb stories just pop into my head about people. For all I know I could be psychic. Or psychotic.

I must have been looking at her chest for too long or with a quizzical expression that she asked, "What's wrong?"

"Your necklace," I said. I couldn't tell her it was stuck to her mole, but I had to say something. "The chain's about an inch too long."

"Too *long*?"

"The pendant. It's competing with the neckline of your blouse. If you just raised it up a little bit, your whole look would be . . . cleaner."

She touched the pendant without looking at it and uttered an annoyed grunt. The pendant fell away from the mole and dropped into its intended place. The other two editors looked at each other, and I got the feeling I had made everyone uncomfortable.

"Other than that," I said, "you're a star! Can I get you guys another drink?"

"No," she said. "We're heading out."

I told them it had been nice chatting with them, which was neither lie nor truth, and headed back to the folding table with a sheet over it serving as the bar. As I waited for the gin and tonic I had ordered from the rented bartender, an actor by his generic good looks, another woman I didn't recognize asked, "How many women at this party have asked you to critique their outfits?"

"Eight or so. Slow night."

"Must be ex*haust*ing." She said it so earnestly I knew she was kidding. With her wavy auburn hair, wide-set blue eyes, and big smile, she reminded me of Cate Blanchett playing Katharine Hepburn.

"You have no idea."

She smiled and modeled her own clothes with a spin. "So, what do you think?"

"You're not nearly as dumpy as everyone says." She gave a fake pout. "I'm kidding. You look fabulous," I said. "I don't even know who you are."

"I'm Cheryl from *Redbook*!"

As it turned out, I did know her. She had interviewed me several times via telephone for a monthly makeover column she wrote about participants on the show. She wasn't one of those writers who asked five thousand questions over the course of an hour for a two-hundred-word story only to painfully misquote me in print. So, she was my new favorite person in the room.

"Am I happy to see you," I said. "Do you want to get out of here by any chance? I'm not sure I can take another minute of this."

"I'm done too," Cheryl said, and we grabbed our things. As we were walking out of the studio, my phone rang. Rick, my on-and-off boyfriend of two years, was calling from our apartment a block away. He asked what time I was coming home and I explained that I was going to grab a drink in the neighborhood with an editor I knew. Never one to pass up the opportunity for a cocktail (he and I weren't too different that way), Rick asked if he could join us and I agreed.

The bars closest to the studio were all filled with bankers who also worked nearby, and I wasn't in the mood for so much heterosexuality. So we walked a few blocks north to a quiet restaurant I had passed several times but never entered. Rick met us there, and before Cheryl and I could finish our drinks, he was bored.

"We should go to Beige," he said.

Beige was gay night at Bowery Bar, where every Tuesday scores of good-looking, immaculately groomed, professional men, many of whom worked in the fashion and entertainment industries, would meet for drinks and act like they were better-looking, more fashionable, and richer than they actually were. When I was in the right mood, I kind of enjoyed it. Cheryl said she would probably just head on home, but Rick convinced her it would be fun. He had that effect on people, convincing them they were on the verge of having a truly spectacular time.

We arrived by taxi a little past 10 p.m. and the bar was busy, not jam-packed but headed that way. Beige usually reached maximum capacity around midnight. While Rick headed to the bar to order us drinks, I said to Cheryl, "Let's play a game."

"OK. Go."

"Your phone rings right now," I said. "It's God. You know this because the caller ID says 'GOD' and because your phone has turned all glowy and sparkly. You answer, and God says, 'CHERYL! YOU MUST SLEEP WITH ONE MAN IN THIS BAR TONIGHT! THE FUTURE OF THE HUMAN RACE DEPENDS ON IT!' Then God hangs up and your phone goes back to normal. Now, look around the room. Who's it gonna be?"

"Can I tell God I'm seeing someone right now?"

"God knows and doesn't care."

"Does God care that no one in this bar wants to sleep with me?"

"Let's pretend a few of them do."

"I choose celibacy."

I was a little miffed that Cheryl wasn't playing by the rules, but I cut her some slack because she was the only woman in a bar full of homos. I was more annoyed that she hadn't asked *me* whom I would sleep with if the human race depended on it, but I was determined to play nonetheless. I scanned the room until I spotted the back of some guy's head that struck me as the most attractive thing I had ever seen. "That one. In the orange stripes," I said.

"What?"

I remembered she wasn't really into the game. "I choose that guy in the stripes. On the other side of the bar. To save the world and all."

"I can't see him from here," Cheryl said.

The funny thing was, I couldn't either. I could see he was tall, about my height, with black hair shorter on the sides than on the top, and wearing an orange, vertically striped, button-front shirt I was fairly certain was by Paul Smith. And then, as if he could hear every word of our conversation, the guy across the room turned around, a full 180 degrees, and looked me directly in the eyes.

I put my hand up to my mouth, so he couldn't read my lips. "He's looking at me," I said to Cheryl. "There's no way he could have heard me, is there?"

"Absolutely not. I can barely hear you and I'm standing right next to you."

"Wow. He's even better-looking from the front."

Rick returned with our cocktails. "I was just talking to a guy at the bar who's a big Broadway producer," he said. "I told him he should cast me in his next show. You should meet him."

"You'll probably have better luck getting cast if you're by yourself," I said. "We'll stay here."

"Suit yourself. I'll thank you when I win my Tony." Rick returned to the producer, I assumed, though I didn't look back to confirm it. I had stopped tracking his whereabouts in bars months ago. This was Rick's milieu, drinking and flirting in a sexually charged atmosphere. With big arms and high cheekbones, he always received considerable attention from strangers, which he enjoyed, too much for my taste. If one drunken college student told him he looked like Jude Law on a Friday night, Rick would be firmly ensconced on Cloud Nine for the remainder of the weekend. If two people over the course of an evening happened to remark upon the same resemblance, he'd talk for a week about moving to Hollywood. The exponential effect of compliments on his mental state intrigued the hell out of me, and I wondered if I secretly paid ten people to tell him he looked like Jude Law over the course of a random day, would his head just explode into a million tiny pieces like a balloon full of glitter?

"You never tell me I'm attractive," he once told me during a fight. I answered, "That's because you seem so convinced of it already." I thought it would sting more than it apparently did, although in retaliation he did call me an "ice queen," which made me laugh.

In a bar filled with men in designer clothes, mostly black fitted jackets, I began to feel a little self-conscious. I hadn't planned on going out for gay drinks and regretted not changing into something more evening-appropriate. It was mid-April and warming up, so I wore a white button-front shirt and a coral sweater by Reiss with two wings printed on the back, one on each shoulder blade. *I'm a harbinger of spring*, I told myself.

(An older woman once called me that when I wore a turquoise paisley tie to a ballroom dancing lesson on a February evening in Boston, and it stuck with me.) It crossed my mind that the cute guy was smiling in my direction because he and his friends were making fun of my outfit, but he was wearing orange, so that would have been a little hypocritical, and he didn't strike me as the type.

Then the cute guy started to walk toward me.

"Oh my God, Cheryl. He's coming over here." My boyfriend was ten feet away from me at the bar. Perhaps I had done something to lead this other—my God, he's really handsome—guy on and now I'd have to awkwardly extricate myself from an inevitable exchange. "Shit. Fuck. What do I do?"

"First, you should wash that mouth out with soap," Cheryl said, nonplussed.

As he maneuvered his way around clusters of chatting men, the cute stranger, I realized, wasn't moving of his own volition. One of the guys he had been speaking with on the other side of the bar was dragging him by the elbow toward me. *He doesn't want to talk to me*, I thought. *Someone is making him talk to me. Oh, the indignity. Please, God, kill me now. Is this retribution for that dumb game? Forgive me my sins because I'm a schmuck.*

His friend placed him directly in front of me with a smirk and asked me, "Are you Clinton Kelly?"

"I am," I said.

"I think you know my friend . . ."

Switch!

At this point, dear reader—as jarring as it may be to your system—I invite you to travel back two years in time with me. I promise we'll return to the man in the orange striped shirt very soon. But first a little more about the path upon which I had been traveling.

I was working as the executive editor of a men's fashion trade magazine called *DNR* ("It's the men's version of *Women's Wear Daily* except it's a weekly," I would say when explaining my career at cocktail parties) and accepting the rare freelance writing assignment when it came up. This particular week, my friend Kevin had asked me if I would write an article and direct a photo shoot about indoor rock climbing for a magazine bankrolled by Philip Morris. I said no, but he talked me into it because we had a history. And because he had money to spend.

For several years I had worked for the custom publishing company that produced the magazine. And even though I wasn't exactly passing out free loosies to twelve-year-olds in the local playground, while employed there I had struggled morally with being a cog—albeit a minuscule one—in the Big Tobacco machine. But the pay was solid for the amount of effort the job required, and the magazine, an oversized action-adventure glossy, was actually quite good. The average person would have assumed it was a newsstand magazine like *Outside* or *Men's Journal,* except there was always a Marlboro ad (usually involving some combination of cowboys, horses, and buttes) on the back, which would have been illegal in a consumer mag. Editorial guidelines forbade any mention of tobacco or smoking, and it was sent without charge to men over the age of twenty-one—approximately 5 million of them—who, somehow or another, had ended up on the Marlboro mailing list.

I once asked a marketing executive how Philip Morris acquired all these names and addresses. She told me, more churlishly than I would have preferred, "A great many people express an interest in Marlboro-branded merchandise." Marlboro-branded merchandise? This information blew my mind. How much does someone need a Marlboro beer koozie that they're willing to tell the tobacco company where they *live*?

I could probably report the story and write it all in one day, Kevin said; it was just one thousand words for which he would pay me *three thousand dollars*. At that point in my life, with credit-card and student-loan debt slowly crushing my soul like an empty milk carton, I would have done a lot worse for a lot less. I had heard the indoor rock wall at Chelsea Piers, a high-end sports complex on Manhattan's West Side, was the best in the city, so I called and asked to speak to someone in their marketing department. The phone rang and a male voice answered.

"This is Damon," the male voice said.

I explained that I was writing a freelance article that would be seen by a lot of people for a magazine he had most certainly never heard of and asked if I could use the wall for a photo shoot and one of the instructors as a source. With a little professional persuasion he agreed, so the next week I took a morning off of work. I figured I would report the story in half a day and write it in one evening.

I wasn't expecting to be so flustered when we met in person. In his white polo shirt and blue chinos, standing in the middle of the weight-training floor, he looked less like a marketing exec than the sexy phys ed teacher I had always wished for in high school.

"Have you ever worked out here?" Damon asked as he escorted me to the climbing area.

"Yeah, just once," I said.

"Why just once?"

"I took a group fitness class," I said. "I forget the name. Extreme Turbo Power or some shit like that. Everyone in it was ridiculously in-shape."

"You look like you're in pretty good shape," he said.

"Thanks, I've been working out. But this was *nuts*. Everyone in the place was ripped. And the class was all running and jumping and free weights. It was too much. I totally barfed."

He opened his eyes wide and I noticed they were green. "You barfed in the class?"

"No, thank God. I had to run to the bathroom in the middle of it. I puked, washed my face, and walked right out the door. Never came back."

He laughed. "I'm sorry," he said. "Maybe you should try another class, on the house."

"Oh, hell no. Still too embarrassed. I'm only here for the money."

When we reached the climbing wall, the photographer was setting up his equipment, which left Damon and me standing there with nothing to do. He asked me how I became a writer, and I told him I got a master's degree in journalism because I thought it would pay the bills. I asked him how he got into marketing for a sports complex, and he told me he had always been an athlete so it seemed a natural fit. At one point, he told me he rowed at Brown and I, completely confused, asked, "Rode what?"

He looked at me as if my head had suddenly turned into a canned ham. "A boat."

"You rode a boat?"

"Yeah. As in crew."

"Oh, rowed!" I said. "I thought you meant you rode— R-O-D-E—like horses or a bicycle or something. Not R-O-W-E-D." I realized that the more I kept talking the more insane I sounded.

As if to save me from further embarrassment, Damon said, "Look, I think you're all set up here. I have to go back to my office, but send me a copy of the story when it's printed." He handed me his business card.

I looked down at it. "Will do, Damon Bayles."

He looked shocked. "You pronounced my name right."

"Damon is a pretty easy name."

"No, Bayles. Most people say Bails. But you said Bay-liss."

"Oh, I didn't even think to pronounce it any other way," I said. "When I was growing up, I used to work at a restaurant called Danfords Inn, and it was on Bayles Dock."

"In Port Jefferson," he said. "Out on Long Island."

"Yeah, that's where I grew up. Do you know it?"

Smiling, he said, "Well, yeah, that's my family's dock. Well, it was. In the 1800s they used to build ships there."

"Get out!"

"I swear." He seemed very serious all of a sudden.

"I worked there all through high school as a busboy," I said, "and as a waiter during summer breaks in college. There was this yacht the restaurant would charter, usually for corporate groups, and I'd have to lug all this food and ice and alcohol across that dock when it was ninety degrees outside. Man, it sucked. How crazy is that? I toiled away for years, sweating my ass off, on your family's dock."

"That is pretty wild," he admitted. "I've been meaning to go out there some time."

"You should," I said. "I could meet you out there for lunch or something."

He smiled a polite smile. "That would be lovely," he said. "Anyway, it seems like you've got everything you need here. I'm going to head back to my desk."

"Gotcha," I said. "Thanks for helping me out with this."

"That's my job!"

When I got back to my office, I decided that I was going to ask Damon out on a date. I just couldn't stop thinking about him. He was smart, funny, athletic, gorgeous, and not an asshole—a breed so rare in New York many assume it's extinct. But I didn't want to ask him out over the phone or e-mail. Too pedestrian. So, I decided to handwrite him a note on my nicest stationery. Maybe that would make me stand out, I hoped, from the mob of homosexuals most certainly clawing at him daily.

I pulled out a note card with my name embossed across the top and wrote: "Can I take you out for coffee sometime?"

It was the me I wanted to be, strong and decisive. A real man's man. But then I decided it was too straightforward, and part of my charm, I hoped, was being kind of a spaz, so I took another note card out of the box and wrote: "I was thinking, maybe, if you had nothing better to do, I could, like, take you out for a coffee, or a tea, or some kind of other beverage if you don't do caffeine. Or not. I mean, I wouldn't want to bother you so . . . ummm . . . give me a call if you feel like it. Or if you're busy I totally understand. Have a nice day. Or a nice life. Or I'll see you soon. Whatever."

I set both note cards down on my desk and tried to decide which one to send. Rambling or direct? Direct or rambling? I must have looked at them for five minutes before I choked. I crammed both into a blue-metallic-lined envelope, along with my business card, addressed it to Damon Bayles at Chelsea Piers, and threw it in the company mail bin.

Four days later I received an e-mail—an e-mail!—that read: "Dear Clinton, I really enjoyed speaking with you. Thank you for your invitation(s), but I'm seeing someone right now. I hope you understand. Maybe we'll bump into each other one of these days. I'll look forward to that. Sincerely, Damon Bayles."

And I thought, *He's lying*. I'm not his type, but he's telling me he's in a relationship because he doesn't want to hurt my feelings. Because I've never been the type to think about what I can't have, I put Damon out of my mind, quite successfully.

The next day I received another significant e-mail, this one from a casting agent asking if I would like to audition for a television makeover show called *What Not to Wear*.

Switch.

Now, where were we again? Oh, that's right. We were in that crowded bar, two years later.

The friend dragging the handsome guy in the orange-striped shirt asked me, "Are you Clinton Kelly?"

"I am," I said.

"I think you know my friend . . ."

"Damon!" I said. "Damon Bayles. How the hell are you?"

When I said that I had put Damon out of my mind, I meant that I had forgotten he existed, forgot what he looked like, everything about him, until that exact moment when it all came flooding back into my brain, my whole being. A switch had been flipped, but not just a switch that triggers memories of platonic encounters of years past. It was a track change. And I *felt* it. It's like being sprayed with a superfine mist of ice-cold water on an excruciatingly hot day, all over your body, all at once. Or standing in a room in which the atmospheric pressure changes so suddenly that you have to take a little breath. Or, I would imagine, watching your baby walk clear across the room, out of the blue, smiling his face off.

"I'm great," he said. "How are you?"

"You know, I'm a big TV star now," I said with a laugh.

"I don't own a television."

He really didn't. That was 2005, and today Damon and I have decided that this story, at least insomuch as it concerns you, is best ended here. I hope you're not offended, but the complete story of "us" just isn't one we want publicly consumed. I will, however, tidy up a few loose ends because I'd hate to leave you hanging. I'm no tease.

Damon was being truthful when he said he was seeing someone. When he called it off with whomever that was (I've never asked), he e-mailed me again to ask me out, but the e-mail bounced back because I had quit my job to embark upon my television journey. He called too, but no one answered. He only had my work information from my business card. And those two note cards I sent him: He kept them. I didn't believe him, but he showed them to me once. I could have died of embarrassment—how ridiculous I was—and yet I wanted to cry from the chest-crushing happiness.

We've been together for eleven years. Sometimes I think about how, if I hadn't accepted the job on *What Not to Wear*, Damon and I would have gotten together much sooner. But would I have been ready? Would he have been ready? Would I have felt the switch—*click!*—the same way I did that night? I'll never know, of course. Unless when I die, some godlike being shows me a map, perhaps an incredibly detailed decision tree of my life, in which all paths lead to Damon. But in this reality, I'm happy with the track I'm on.

CLINTON FOR PRESIDENT!

Joan Rivers released a comedy album in 1983 called *What Becomes a Semi-Legend Most?* I literally have no idea how an 8-track of it found its way into my first car a few years later, but I listened to it constantly for a month or so, until I stopped laughing at the jokes out of familiarity. Today, I remember little about her routine, except one short bit that still resonates with me:

"Drugs," Joan says. "I don't do *drugs*. But every once in a while I sprinkle a little Fresca on a panty shield. Perks me right up."

For thirty years I used a variation of that line at countless parties when offered a toke of this or a snort of that. "Nah, I don't feel like doing a bong hit right now, I just reapplied Fresca to my panty shield and, dude, I am trippin' *balls*." I don't think anyone ever laughed, just gave me that aloof, slightly confused look I usually reserve for people with really short bangs or novelty hosiery.

I'm just not that into drugs, despite the fact that I've done my fair share of them. It's a control thing, really. I know exactly what I'm going to feel like after two margaritas (horny and bitchy) or three gin and tonics (horny and exhibitionistic), but with drugs you never know what kind of high—or low—you're going to have. The last time I chased half a joint with a Vicodin I ended up screaming obscenities at a leprechaun because he was shitting pennies all over my living room. The next day the woman who lived across the hall told me she thought I had been babysitting until she heard me yell, "If I see one more coin come out of your ass, so help me God!" at which point she assumed I had a "special friend" over.

That was 2004 and I haven't done recreational drugs since, yet I'm kind of intrigued by people who do. Do they use because they *want* to get out of their own heads, or do they *need* to? And where are these people going that's so great, because I never got there. I did have a fantasy for a while about composing a series of mystical essays after ingesting different substances. You know, one Saturday chew a few 'shrooms and write about the meaning of life; the next, take some LSD and see if I can channel Buddha. And so on and so on, until the only drugs I haven't done are crank and bath salts. I chickened out, *mostly because I don't want to die*, but on some level I think it would be fun.

So, recently I tried a much safer, somewhat legal version.

I was in San Francisco after a trip to Los Angeles for work and I asked a friend of mine—Renée—with a medicinal marijuana prescription for her "anxiety" to buy me one dose of an edible, because I was conducting an experiment. She asked what the experiment entailed and I told her: "I just want to try writing while high to see if it's any better or worse than what I come up with when I'm sober." Renée, who was also writing a book at the time, said she had attempted the same thing to no avail. Every time she tried to write while high, she got a case of the fuck-its, closed her computer, and watched TV or ate cookie dough. She suggested that I take a marijuana gummy, and she would stay with me, sober, and interview me, while recording the whole thing on her phone. I said it sounded like a plan.

On a Sunday night in mid-May, Renée came to my hotel room. I chewed and swallowed one THC-infused gummy bear and this is what transpired:

RENÉE: So, what do you want to talk about?

ME: I'm not sure this thing is working. Are you sure you didn't give me a regular gummy bear?

RENÉE: I'm sure.

ME: In Germany they call them GOO-me bears.

RENÉE: Ya.

ME: Shit. I forgot to tell Damon we were doing this.

RENÉE: Do you want to call him now?

ME: No. What if he gets mad at me?

RENÉE: Do you think he would?

ME: He doesn't like *los drugas*.

RENÉE: *Las drogas*.

ME: I took French. Is my forehead shining? I feel like my forehead is shining.

RENÉE: A little.

ME: [Looking in mirror] I look like shit. You know, once you start wearing makeup, it's hard to get used to seeing your own face without it. Don't tell anybody, but sometimes—well, always, actually—I fill in my eyebrows just a bit, with a MAC pencil. They've gotten sparse with age. You know Tony Goldwyn?

RENÉE: The actor?

ME: Yeah, he looks good without eyebrows. He's got strong features to carry the rest of his face. I don't. My face is so oval.

RENÉE: Isn't that supposed to be the ideal face shape?

ME: For women! When was the last time you saw a guy and were like, "I just wanna hop on that sexy oval face, ya big stud."

RENÉE: You may have a point. But I still like your face.

ME: Thanks. You know, sometimes I think I may be invisible to birds.

RENÉE: What makes you say that?

ME: They've been flying at me, like I'm not there. But then at the last minute, they dart away. It's like my bird force field has gotten thinner or something. I should Google that. What if my fucking aura is fizzling out? Birds can see things we can't see, you know. The birds used to be able to see my aura and they could steer clear of it. Now, it's barely there. Can't see it until you're right up in it.

RENÉE: Do you feel like your aura is fizzling out?

ME: Sometimes.

RENÉE: Why?

ME: Old age. I don't know. Stacy [London] and I had our aura photographed once a long time ago. We were in a New Age shop shooting part of the show in our first season. We were in Nashville. We had matching gold auras. The guy who owned the shop said we were practically angels or some shit.

RENÉE: Well, you were helping people.

ME: When was the last time an angel helped you by suggesting you wear dark-wash jeans and ballet flats?

RENÉE: Do you ever miss that show?

ME: Next question.

RENÉE: When did—

ME: I should have another gummy because I don't think this one is on.

RENÉE: You're OK with the one.

ME: Prolly. You know what this country needs?

RENÉE: What?

ME: A makeover. I think we'd all be happier if we looked cuter. [*laughs*] And had some GOO-me bears. When I'm president, I will make America fabulous again.

RENÉE: Ah, you want to be president.

ME: Well, it's obvious I'm the most qualified. To make people fabulous. The dream is real.

RENÉE: And what exactly does being fabulous mean in this context, Candidate Kelly?

ME: A chicken in every pot and—what's that expression?—a car in every garage. A pasture-raised, organic chicken. And an electric car. I'd like it if the chickens were killed really fast and didn't see it coming, and if the cars were colorful, like in the old days. Just a rainbow of cars, plus pink ones. Pink isn't in the rainbow, but pink cars are cute. Now all the cars are black and white. Some are red. Did you ever notice that everyone driving a Nissan Maxima is an asshole?

RENÉE: Will you mention that on the campaign trail?

ME: I'm not going on the campaign trail. That seems exhausting. And all that food they make you eat. Gross. Do you want to order room service? They do a nice cheese platter here. It comes with quince jelly.

RENÉE: Maybe later. We're on a roll here. Let's discuss some of your specific policies.

ME: If you insist.

RENÉE: Transgendered individuals in restrooms. What are your thoughts on that topic?

ME: To be honest, I don't know what all the hubbub is about. Does it really matter who's peeing in the next stall, and whether they're wearing a ball gown or overalls? I find the whole process so revolting, I just want to get in and out with as little fanfare as possible.

RENÉE: But people are concerned about the children. Specifically, little girls using a public restroom with a man.

ME: Why the fuck are you letting your little girl enter a public restroom alone anyway? That's neglect. Your kids should be interacting with absolutely no one in a public toilet, whether they have a penis, a vagina, both, or neither. Quite frankly, I think we need sweeping change in the way we publicly relieve ourselves. I dream of a future in which public restrooms are gender neutral. Hear me out on this. You enter the restroom, which would have a series of completely private rooms with a hole on the floor. You do your business, a onesie or a twosie into the hole, wipe as necessary, and leave. When you exit, the door closes behind you and the entire room is sprayed down with warm water and a biodegradable disinfectant. So the next person who enters gets a completely clean, odor-free toilet experience. That can happen. If there are people smart enough to make all these goddamn Snapchat filters, someone can figure out a new toilet system.

RENÉE: Wouldn't it be expensive to convert all existing bathrooms to the kind you've described?

ME: It's a jobs program! Someone has to make and install these toilets. Pronounced "toilette," by the way. And we'll start with the unemployed. Oh, and I'll raise taxes. Imagine, for an extra twenty dollars a year, you could be guaranteed a safe, hygienic pee whenever you wanted one.

RENÉE: What about your stance on abortion?

ME: This is another thing that's pissing me off. Nobody *wants* an abortion. Kind of the way nobody wants to use a public restroom, but multiply that by about a thousand. There would be a shit-ton less abortion if we made it easier to get contraception in this country. I don't know why there aren't buckets of free condoms in every classroom in America. Oh, when I'm president, I will institute a Contraception On-Demand program the *second* I am sworn in.

RENÉE: Can you explain what you mean by Contraception On-Demand?

ME: Drones. Contraception is delivered to your front door whenever you want it. Have a hot date? Tap a button on your phone, and—*bam*—a box of condoms, spermicidal jelly, sponges, whatever you want. It's at your front door. And if you made a mistake last night, tap an icon on the screen of your phone— I guess you'd need the geo-location function turned on—and in five minutes you could literally be showered with morning-after pills, like Skittles. Taste the rainbow and flush out that zygote you created six hours ago before it turns into anything.

RENÉE: That seems like a lot of pills just lying around on the sidewalk.

ME: Well, maybe we could use small drones, like the size of hummingbirds, that drop a single pill right into your hand. Or we could train actual humming-birds. Wouldn't that be cute?

RENÉE: What about men? It seems like the onus is on women here.

ME: Oh, hell, no. I want to incentivize men to have vasectomies. Reversible ones, of course. You come to the local hospital. *Snip snip*, no charge. When you're ready to responsibly procreate, we sew your vas def-erens right back up again. Nobody's inconvenienced.

RENÉE: What's the incentive?

ME: A guarantee of no child support payments. And we can throw in a free pizza with all the toppings. Oh my God, how awesome would pizza be right now?

RENÉE: I can't see a male-dominated Congress passing any of these laws.

ME: Me either. That's why my second slogan is, "Don't be a dick, Vote with your vagina." I don't know why women aren't furious that they're not at least 50 per-cent of the House and Senate. And there should be more gays in there, too, now that I think about it. Let's put more homos in da House! The parties will be much better. And slim-leg pants. What is with the old dudes still shopping at Men's Wearhouse? Even Paul Ryan. I don't like him, but he's kind of good-looking. The jackets are too long. The pants are all big and baggy. I don't like it. I did like his beard, when he had it.

RENÉE: How does it feel to be the first gay man run-ning for president?

ME: I'm pretty sure a couple of gays have run or maybe even been president. I'm just the first to admit it. That being said, it feels fine. I could do without the e-mails telling me God hates me.

RENÉE: Does that happen?

ME: I'll get one tweet a month or one Facebook message where some asshole is quoting Leviticus to me and telling me I'm going to burn in hell. I don't believe in hell, so I'm not too worried about it. It's like someone saying to me, "You're gonna go to Wally World." Um, no, that's from a movie, dipshit.

RENÉE: Does religion not play a big role in your life?

ME: It doesn't. I don't really see the point, to be honest. I can have a relationship with God without all the middlemen. If I shut my eyes and say, "Hey, God, thanks for all the good stuff around me," what difference does it make if I'm in a church or on the subway? Did you know I'm kind of obsessed with the New York City subway system? There are few things in life that make me as happy as seeing an Arab, some Hasidic Jews, assorted blacks, whites, Hispanics, Asians, gays, and European tourists peacefully coexisting on an uptown express train in the middle of the afternoon.

RENÉE: When did you realize you were gay?

ME: Hmm. I can't point to any moment in particular. But I do remember not feeling quote-unquote "normal," whatever that means. Just less aggressive, drawn more to the beautiful things in life. I remember being around seven years old and throwing rocks in our suburban neighborhood. That's what kids, boys especially, did back then, roam around looking for things to do and throw. The rule was be home before it gets dark. Can you imagine telling your child that now? You'd be shamed out of suburbia. But it was a different world. The entire neighborhood was the playground, with mothers everywhere keeping eyes on kids who were not necessarily their own. At one point—it must have been early summer, because I wore jeans and a short-sleeved shirt, I remember it clearly—I found myself atop a mound of dirt. Which seemed substantial to me at the time, but may have only been a few feet high. The boys were throwing rocks into a nearby bush, and so I picked up some rocks and began to do the same. "Why are we throwing rocks into that bush?" I asked one of the other kids. "Because there's a rabbit in there," he said. Horrified, I dropped the rocks I held in my hand and ran down the dirt mound and stood in front of the bush. I threw my hands in the air, waved them the way one might surrender to opposing forces, and yelled, "Stop! You might hurt the rabb—" when a rock hit me so hard over the right eye that I fell back into the bush and blacked out.

When I came to, maybe five minutes later, my eye was filled with blood. I closed it and looked to the mound of dirt, where a half-dozen boys had been standing, and saw that it was now empty. It was the first time I had ever felt profoundly alone, deserted. I rose to my feet, my head aching and my stomach wobbly, and heard the pack of boys yelling. They were coming my way with my mother in tow. "Mrs. Kelly, Mrs. Kelly," they yelled. Because she was Mrs. Kelly then. "Clint's eyeball's hanging out." And I had an image of myself as a deformed monster, my beautiful blue eyes, which even complete strangers complimented me and my mother on, were ruined forever. Terri grabbed me by the shoulders and looked at my face. "Is my eyeball hanging out?" I asked. "No," she said, "but you've got a bad cut. I'm taking you to the emergency room." "I was trying to save a rabbit," I said. She was holding my arm as we walked through the neighbors' backyards to our house. "Well, now you're going to the hospital," she said.

I didn't know if she was mad, inconvenienced, or frightened. Maybe a combination of all three, plus some emotions I wasn't yet aware of. Anyway, that was probably when I realized I wasn't like the other boys. But of course it wasn't sexual back then. I don't think I was sexually attracted to men until high school. Not that I acted upon it. That didn't happen until college in Boston.

RENÉE: Do you think the country is ready for a gay president?

ME: Hell no. [laughs]

RENÉE: What's so funny?

ME: It's ridiculous, isn't it? The country would go apoplectic. People talk about the sanctity of marriage between a man and a woman. Damon and I are completely monogamous, but a heterosexual couple can swing every weekend, and somehow their marriage is more sacred in the eyes of God than mine. I've got a real problem with Chinese restaurant–style religion. "I'll make two choices from Leviticus and three from Deuteronomy, and ignore the rest because they inconvenience me."

RENÉE: That probably won't endear you to a substantial portion of the American electorate.

ME: Probably not.

RENÉE: So what do you think your chances of winning are?

ME: I'd calculate them to be somewhere in the neighborhood of zero. But if I really thought I'd win, I wouldn't run. That job's gotta suck. I'd like to go to bed now if that's OK with you.

RENÉE: Sweet dreams, Mr. President.

YOU YOUNG, ME RESTLESS

The bare masts of sailboats rock back and forth in Biscayne Bay like metronomes keeping different tempos. The sky is clear, thank God, except for a few puffy clouds to the south. It's been raining for days, making me grumpy as hell. I'm hopeful my foul mood will lift today, but I'm not placing any bets; it's only eight o'clock in the morning. From my seat at the table— Damon usually sits to my left, but he's not here now—I look directly out the sliding glass doors of our terrace into the tops of palm trees. Sometimes an iguana riding the fronds will stare back at me, but not today. To my right is an unobstructed view of the water and, across the bay, the cranes that relieve the enormous flat-decked cargo ships of their burdens in the port of Miami.

We bought this apartment to escape the winter doldrums of the Northeast. I need to see blue and green, and birds that aren't pigeons, I told Damon when attempting, successfully, to convince him we should shuffle some of our money around. We'll probably sell it soon, now that I've renovated and redecorated it. I need a new project.

My hand is curled around the mug that holds my cappuccino. Despite how pretty it is, with its pink-and-white arabesque pattern, the cup reminds me that I am a failure. I designed it along with coordinating plates and bowls for Macy's, but the line was not reordered. Sales were fine, the buyers said. Not great. There's no room in the retail world for *fine*, I've discovered. I wonder if I should have tried harder to promote them and give a little shrug.

The caffeine seems to be waking me up, albeit slowly, so I decide to check my social media accounts. Usually someone is out there, somewhere, wanting advice on what shoes to wear to an upcoming wedding or how to break into the world of television. I enjoy answering them. Nothing of any interest on Twitter today, just a few people saying nice things about my recipes on *The Chew*. I tap the little heart icon to let them know they've been heard. On Instagram, I discover some old messages in my inbox. (I didn't even know I had an Instagram inbox.) There's one from six months ago that catches my eye, from a fan who's attached a screen grab of a young, fairly pretty comedian's post. She, this comedian I've never heard of, has taken several images of me on a recent episode and arranged them into a collage and written a caustic caption about what a terrible haircut I have. Many of her followers have chimed in, some with LOLs, others with derisive comments about my face or sexuality.

It stings a bit, considerably less than the things I read about myself online thirteen years ago, when I first began my television career. *He's so ugly he's so gay he's not funny he's got no style.* The usual stuff. Over time, skin grows thicker and one learns not to go self-searching. I consider composing a private message to this comedian, informing her that she will never find love and most probably die alone because she's a shitty human being. But then I realize she'll figure that out on her own anyway. Best not to waste a moment of this beautiful day fanning online flames.

Perhaps Facebook will be less bitchy. I log in to my fan page and see that overnight I have received dozens of private messages written in Spanish and Portuguese, languages I don't speak. After copying and pasting their e-mails in Google Translate, I learn these people, mostly young men and women in their twenties, are raving about a show called *Amor en Linea* or "Love Online." It's what executives at Discovery networks have apparently renamed *Love at First Swipe*, a makeover show I created, executive produced, and starred in for TLC. After one season, the president of TLC told me she chose not to renew the show because it "couldn't find an audience." Evidently it has found an audience—in South America, but at this point it is too late. I close my laptop.

Suddenly, a fast-moving blur out the window to my right catches my eye. I quickly turn my head and see a bird flying directly toward me and—*bang!*—right into the center of the hurricane-proof glass. The suddenness of the sight and sound causes me to jump in my seat, my heart racing a bit. I get up and look out the window. Nothing. Just the same blue skies and green palm treetops.

Maybe the bird survived, the optimist in me thinks. I pace around the apartment for a few minutes before I decide to go downstairs and see for myself. I put on my flip-flops, take the elevator down one flight, and as I walk through the lobby toward the courtyard, I realize that if the bird is not dead, he may be crippled. What would I do if I found him with a broken wing or a shattered beak? I wonder. How horrible it would be to see an innocent creature suffer. Now I hope he is dead.

I search the ground directly below our dining room window. Nothing. No tiny avian carcass. No peeping invalid. Not so much as a weightless feather lying in the mulch. The little guy must have hit his head and shaken it off. I am relieved.

And then I find him, dead and curled up in a philodendron. He is lying in what strikes me as the sweet spot of the plant, where the firm stem meets the floppy leaf—a little hollow like the palm of a cupped hand. He is roughly the size of a sparrow and the gray of a dove. He is not a bird one would look at and say, "Now *there* is a gorgeous animal." Yet I find his abject simplicity attractive. He looks like the type who, when alive, may have been content with what little he had. What would that be like, I wonder, to be happy with less, to live simply? I was once, I did once. I think. The past is getting hazy. All I know is that now my little bird has nothing, except what appears to be a comfortable spot to begin his inevitable return to unconstrained atoms, some of which may float to the sky, or in my window.

Back upstairs, I notice a very faint stain on the glass; I assume I left a smudge, perhaps with my hand or forehead, when looking for the bird earlier. But the smudge is on the outside, left behind by the bird, an almost perfect three-inch imprint of itself, head turned to the side, wings spread, eye open. A little bird ghost. I consider taking a picture to show Damon, but decide that the impression is too faint. And for some reason to do so seems like a breach of trust. Evidence of the bird's stupidity will remain my secret, until a rainstorm washes it away.

I need to leave this place, have some breakfast elsewhere. I decide on a nearby restaurant situated amid cycling and yoga studios and a boot camp–style gym. Some class or other must have recently ended because everyone around me is in perfect physical condition and wearing athletic wear.

I sit down at a table near the window and contemplate the menu. I should have the oatmeal because I'm trying to lose ten pounds, but when the waitress arrives, I order the combo platter of scrambled eggs with cheese, a biscuit, and potatoes. At the table next to me, a blonde with perfectly beachy curls is drinking a green smoothie. She must be a model. She has the most flawless golden skin I have ever seen. I don't know how she could possibly achieve such a color, except by sitting in the sun for no less or more than seven minutes a day, every day, and taking regular baths in rainbows and the blood of angels. She has a little star tattooed on the inside of her left wrist, I assume to remind herself that she is one. Her sunglasses cover three-quarters of her face.

The man she's with is not a man, despite the fact that he is the perfect specimen of manhood. He is a boy, at least he must be because he has not a wrinkle or a pore, not so much as a freckle. And where did he get all the muscles? One must work for those, right? And yet he looks as though he's never worked at anything a day in his life.

I was this young once, wasn't I? Certainly never Roman-statue-quality like these two, but cute enough. Right? Except . . . I didn't feel cute at the time. There was always something wrong with me. My jaw wasn't square enough, my shoulders not strong enough, my clothes not cool enough. This couple is literally everything I was not.

I *despise* them. No. I despise the fact that I want to *be* them. Just for a day. Either one of them. Or both of them. I don't care. I want to ride a bicycle shirtless. I want to dance in a club with strangers lusting after me. I want to look in the mirror after taking a shower and not wonder who will eventually win the battle to destroy my body: Father Time set on degrading the strands of my DNA, or Mother Earth with her incessant pull of gravity.

I want to live to be one hundred years old for the sole purpose of tracking these two down. I will find them sitting in a café like this one and reach out both of my withered hands. I will touch them on the slack, mottled skin of their forearms.

"I knew this would happen," I will tell them.

"What would happen, old-timer?" the boy will say. He will be in his late seventies now.

"The skin. The hair," I'll say. "It's gone. You have been betrayed. You thought you wouldn't be, but you were."

"Go away, old man," she will say, brushing her hand at me. Her star tattoo is gone. Perhaps she had it lasered off when it began to blur and fade.

"I hate to bother you," the girl says. She is speaking to me.

I am snapped out of my trance. "No bother," I tell her.

"Are you Clinton Kelly?"

"I am."

"I'm sure you hear this all the time, but I love you." She has taken off her sunglasses so that she can look me in the eyes.

I am surprised that a human being this beautiful even knows of my existence in the world. It is always strange to hear *I love you* from a stranger. My instinct is to say *I love you* in return, but that seems to me disingenuous, condescending. What I really want to say is, *You know some of me, and I'm glad you love that part of me but if you knew all of me you might not even like me. Nevertheless, I hope that someday a stranger tells you how much they love you, because it feels pretty good.*

"That's very nice of you to say. Thank you."

We talk some more. Her name is Maddy, short for Madeleine. Her friend's name is Preston. He does not know who I am. I tell her there's a song I love called "Madeleine" from a musical called *Jacques Brel Is Alive and Well and Living in Paris*. She suggests we look it up online right now and listen to it. There is no need, I say. I have it on my phone.

"Let's hear it!" she says excitedly.

It takes me a minute to find the song and I begin to feel self-conscious, they probably think I don't know how to use modern technology. I press play and the song begins. The four-part harmony sounds like a barbershop quartet sung in double tempo.

"That is old school," Preston says before the first verse is over. Maddy shushes him. Other patrons in the restaurant are looking at us, and I realize I am being self-indulgent, playing a song written in the sixties, probably before the parents of this young couple were born: "I'm waiting for Madeleine / In front of the picture show."

"You don't need to listen to the rest," I say, hitting the pause button. "Basically, the guy's in love with Madeleine, but she keeps standing him up. He waits for her in the rain and catches a cold. The end."

"Do you think Madeleine is toying with him?" she asks. It's a question I hadn't thought of before, but I get the impression she, this real live Madeleine, is toying with *me*. She's being flirty, charming, staring me in the eyes with a broad close-lipped smile. Is she interested in any of this, honestly? Or is this the way she might talk to any old man feeding pigeons on a park bench?

"Perhaps," I say. "I don't usually consider Madeleine. I'm more focused on the guy getting soaking wet in front of the movie theater."

"Maybe she's watching him from the window of the coffee shop across the street," Maddy says.

"That's mean. Maybe his cold turns into a really bad case of pneumonia," I say.

"Maybe she rushes to his bedside and declares her undying love for him," Maddy says, "and they live happily ever after."

"They'd probably be in their midsixties by now."

"I can see them holding hands and walking through a little park in Paris." She turns her gaze to Preston. She touches his hand and gives it a gentle squeeze. It's her signal to him that they should get going.

Preston removes some cash from his wallet and places it on the table, and before they depart we exchange pleasantries. I'm doubtful I will ever see these two again, but even if I do I will probably do my best to avoid them. I feel like some kind of youth vampire in their presence and I don't like it. I fear I just might bite one of their necks if it would make me look five years younger.

While I eat my breakfast—everything my doctor has suggested I avoid due to my elevated cholesterol levels—the waitress clears the green-smoothie glass and white ceramic bowl, which contained oatmeal, I think, from the empty table and resets it. I ask for my check and extract a credit card from my pocket.

The host seats a woman in her midthirties and her young daughter, who is about four, where Preston and Maddy had been sitting just a few minutes before. Perhaps they were never really there in the first place. The mother's eyes are glued to her cellphone, the girl's wander around the room and land on me. I smile politely and lift my hand in a halfhearted wave. I usually don't like children, but this one seems quiet and introspective, the way I like to believe I was fortysomething years ago.

She sticks out her tongue at me, just a little, probably because she knows she might get in trouble should her mother catch her. I return the gesture, very quickly, I don't particularly want to be reprimanded by her mother either.

The little girl shrugs and for the first time in days, I laugh. Not too loudly, because it really isn't all that funny, but the way she lifts her shoulders and rolls her eyes reminds me of something an old lady might do while saying, "Eh, who cares."

Yes! That's it, kid. So, I'm getting old. So, I've had a few failures. So, I'm gonna die, just like everyone else in this damn room. Eh, who cares.

TEXTBOOK PENIS

My penis is technically perfect.

I know what you're thinking: Every guy says his penis is perfect. Well, that may or may not be true, but mine really is. Seriously. I'm not trying to be braggy or anything, just honest. Many things about me are not even close to being perfect. For example, my eyes are slightly too close together, I have a patch of curly hair only on the left side of my head, and no matter how much weight I lift at the gym, I still have forearms skinnier than Tori Spelling's. We all have our crosses to bear, but luckily, my dick isn't one of them.

By the time I was fifteen, I began asking myself the same questions every guy asks himself. Does this thing look like what it's supposed to look like? Is this thing the right size? And what about those two other things? Are they supposed to just hang out like that all day? And why do they always seem to be moving when I'm just lying there in bed? (I still don't know the answer to that last one. Balls are so weird.)

Most teenage boys compare wieners in the locker room, I guess, or maybe they talk to their guy friends about this kind of stuff. But I had successfully avoided all team sports and we weren't forced to shower after gym class, so I wasn't seeing too many soapy willies other than my own. Plus, my best friends were girls, and they only talked about their boobs and periods. I guess I could have gone to Mike with my questions, but talking to him about penises would have reminded me that he was boning Terri, and I would rather have eaten batteries than imagine that.

So one Saturday I got on my bike and rode to the public library to do a little research on male genitalia. The sexuality books were on the second floor in the science section, so I meandered through the stacks, pulling random textbooks here and there, just so no one who might cross paths with me would think I was a pervert.

"Hmmmm . . . *Advanced Organic Chemistry*. That looks interesting! I'll take it. *Animal Husbandry*, sounds fascinating. Let me grab that one too. *Human Reproduction*. Ha-ha-ha. I already know everything there is to know about that topic, but let me flip through it just for a few laughs and cocks. I just *looove* the library."

I sat in the far corner of the reading room, back to the wall like a mob boss, praying that no one from school would enter. If they did, my plan was to discreetly place the reproduction book in the trash can next to my seat, feign a coughing fit, and slip out the front door. And if I saw a librarian approach at any point, I would leap from my chair, heading her off at the pass, and ask her if she needed any help organizing the card catalog. "I just hate when people take the cards out and put them back in the wrong spot. The Dewey Decimal System only works when we all do our part." As though 95 percent of people going near the human anatomy books weren't pre-Internet-era pubescent boys.

As it turned out, I was uninterrupted in my research, and let me tell you, that book changed my life, especially the four-color, incredibly detailed illustration of the erect male penis. Because . . . it looked exactly like mine! I'm not kidding. It was like I had modeled for it. I had never felt prouder in my entire life. Not only was my penis a normal penis, it was The Penis. The writers of that textbook could have chosen any other penis in the entire world. But they didn't. They chose my penis. It was the penis that all other penises should and would be compared to. It was the penis that inspired people to learn more about penises. It was the quintessential! The archetypal! The perfect textbook penis!

And it belonged to me.

That made me feel pretty damn good, as you can imagine. It provided me with a confidence that eventually led to a superiority complex, which culminated in a thriving television career.

Almost twenty years later, it's New Year's Day and my boyfriend at the time, Rick, and I are waking up in the Peninsula hotel in Bangkok.

At 10 a.m., the sun was strong and light was flooding into the room around the curtains. I stretched, mildly hungover, and reached for the bottle of water on the nightstand. I took a few glugs and decided to take in the view of the Chao Phraya River. Swinging my legs over the side of the bed, I looked down and, gadzooks, there it was.

The spot was about the size of a nickel and almost as round. Light raspberry in color, it was located smack dab in the middle of the glans, or head, of my penis. In fact, it was so perfectly situated that its placement seemed intentional, as if put there by a graphic designer with a penchant for symmetry and a really fucked-up sense of humor.

How did this happen? I tried to remember if I had done anything that might have caused a circular irritation, but my recollection of the previous night was hazy. It was New Year's Eve, so we went out to a gay nightclub, which was packed and smelled like chicken satay and Drakkar Noir. We had a few drinks . . . well, maybe more than a few . . . What was I missing? Think, Clinton, think!

In my frantic attempt to fill in the blank, I came up with the only logical explanation: I must have had a sticker on my penis. Yes, that made perfect sense. At some point in the evening I must have whipped out my penis and let someone put a smiley face sticker on it. Or maybe I had peeled the label off a Chiquita banana and thought it would look good on my wang. And now I was experiencing an allergic reaction to the adhesive. Simple as that.

I shook Rick, who was asleep in a tangle of white sheets and pillows next to me.

"Hey. Wake up!"

He groaned, as people do when they're hungover and someone is attempting to dislocate their shoulder.

"I need you to wake up. Now," I commanded.

He squinted, annoyed. His voice was gravelly. "What?"

"Did I stick a sticker on my dick?"

His annoyance gave way to confusion, which infuriated the hell out of me. It was a really simple question, asked in English, his first and only language. I didn't think I could be any clearer, but I tried. "My dick," I said. "Did I—or anyone else—put anything on it? Like a sticker of some sort?"

Still nothing.

"Rick, there is a spot. On my penis. Do you know how it got there?"

"What kind of spot?" he asked. Finally we were getting somewhere.

"It's red. On the tip."

"Let me see."

Reluctantly, I showed Rick my dick. He turned on the nightstand lamp and regarded my willy as though it had just fallen to earth during a meteor shower. Then it hit me: I had an STD! I just knew something like this would happen. Our relationship wasn't an open one, but it wasn't exactly closed either. There was a matchbox in the door, I was fond of saying.

"You did this to me!" I accused while he was rolling my penis between his thumb and forefinger. In retrospect, I'll admit it's pretty stupid to accuse someone of giving you gonorrhea when he has direct access to your balls.

He looked up, his face a combination of righteous indignation and hurt feelings. "Me?"

"You gave me something," I said. "I don't know what, but when I find out I'm going to kill you."

The entire time Rick and I dated, I knew on some level that we shouldn't be together. When you regularly want to murder someone, usually it's a sign that things aren't "meant to be." But I tried to convince myself we had things in common. For example, we were both Pisces. We were both tall. And we both lived uptown. Surely, relationships have been built on less.

What probably kept us together was Rick's ability to produce a level of rage in me so profound it actually inspired out-of-body experiences. And for that I give him credit, because I'm pretty even-keeled as humans go. The uppermost limit of my mania is jumping for joy after winning party games; on the low end I get mildly depressed for three consecutive days each year, during which time I tell my agent I'm quitting TV to open an animal shelter or sell mosaic tables. But with Rick I was psychotic, like batshit crazy. I threw drinks at him in bars. I stormed out of restaurants. I yelled at the top of my lungs in hotel hallways: "I saw you! I saw you with your fucking tongue down his throat! I'm not blind, you fucking fuck of a fuck!"

"Calm down," Rick said. "It's not an STD. I bet it will go away on its own in a few days. We're on vacation. Let's try to forget about it."

Rick was sort of right. The spot faded a little, but it didn't quite go away. Two days later, we visited a beautiful hotel in Krabi, Thailand, where Jared Leto was also staying, and two days after that we had delicious dim sum in Hong Kong. But truth be told, I wasn't really myself that whole trip. It's hard to have fun on vacation when your dick looks like the Japanese flag.

As soon as we got back to New York, I made an appointment with a dermatologist, a nice-enough guy who was on my health-care plan with an office near my apartment.

"What brings you here today, Mr. Kelly?" he asked.

"Well," I said, "I have what I think is a rash."

"Yes, I see you wrote that on your form. Where is this rash?"

I had rehearsed what I was going to say, not everything, just the part about not using the word "dick" while talking to a doctor. *Don't say dick. Don't say dick.* "Penis. It's on my penis."

He turned and began to put on a pair of latex gloves. Maybe it was just my imagination, but I'm pretty sure I heard him exhale while his back was turned, the kind of exhale that is usually accompanied by an eye roll. "I'll need you to drop your pants and underwear, please, and sit on the edge of the table." I did as requested, and as luck would have it, this guy had the air-conditioning in his exam room set to absolute zero. I tried thinking dirty thoughts to perk things up, but there wasn't enough time for any major change. It was all happening so fast.

"Let's see what's up with this little guy." He turned my penis between his thumb and forefinger. (More people than usual were doing that lately.) I turned to face the wall only to be confronted by a poster I remembered from the last time I went to the dermatologist, the one detailing the different types of skin cancer.

I blurted: "Do I have penis cancer?"

"No, you do not have penile cancer, but this is very interesting. It looks like something called a fixed drug reaction. It's pretty rare." His eyes met mine. "Have you been on antibiotics lately?"

"No. No I haven't." And then it hit me. "Oh, wait. I took some Cipro."

"Why were you on Cipro?" he asked.

"My mother gave them to me during that anthrax scare."

In late October 2001, a Bronx woman died of inhaled anthrax, which she contracted while at work in the Manhattan Eye, Ear, and Throat Hospital, just three blocks away from my apartment. It was a sad and scary time to live in New York, the Twin Towers having been attacked the previous month. People were waiting for the next terrorist attack. They were afraid to open their mail, and the news media got everyone riled up about the availability of Cipro, the antibiotic used to fight anthrax infection. "Drug manufacturers can't make enough Cipro!" they screamed. "We're all gonna die! Only Cipro can save us!" It was the typical bullshit, but it was difficult not to get at least a little caught up in it.

Somehow, amid the hysteria and stockpiling, Terri managed to get her hands on a case of Cipro. How she did it, I have no idea. My parents are crazy—and a little scary—like that. If my sisters or I need something really important, it shows up and nobody asks questions.

"That was over a year ago. Is your mother a doctor?"

"No. I was in Thailand and I was afraid of getting food poisoning."

I don't know where I got the idea to use Cipro as a prophylaxis against traveler's diarrhea, but it seemed like a good idea at the time. The bottle of Cipro Terri had sent me after the anthrax scare sat in my medicine cabinet for more than a year, never opened, but I took it to Asia, just in case I needed a powerful antibiotic. Before Rick and I left on our vacation, my friend Patty got me all worked up about crazy Asian stomach bugs. She told me that during her trip to Thailand, she had to literally *jump off a boat in the middle of the ocean to poo in the water* (which is literally my worst nightmare!) because she had eaten some bad shrimp. So when I noticed a dead dog floating down the river not five feet away from me in Bangkok—while I was eating fried shrimp from a food cart, no less—I immediately popped a couple of football-size pills and said little prayer to the travel gods that the contents of my large intestine not liquefy.

Evidently, the travel gods have a wicked sense of humor.

The dermatologist shook his head, picked up his pen, and began to write in my file while lecturing me. "Mr. Kelly, you should never take any medicine that was not prescribed to you by a physician for a specific purpose." I was actually being scolded while my pants and underwear were bunched around my ankles. I apologized, and he explained to me that I'm allergic to a family of antibiotics called quinolones and should I ingest them ever again I could expect another spot in the same place. This "reaction" would eventually disappear on its own. But before that

happened, he said, "I'd like to show your penis to my students."
He taught dermatology to medical interns.

"Look," I said, "there is absolutely no way I'm showing my
dick—er, penis—to a bunch of doctor wannabes. I'm on television!" Then I had to explain that I was hosting a show on TLC
and the last thing I needed was someone posting a picture of my
spotted dick on the Internet.

"Well, I could take a picture," he suggested, "and nobody
would know it was you. I contribute to several dermatology
journals and I'm writing a textbook."

My penis in a medical textbook? With a spot on it?

"Oh, hell no!" I could not get my pants on fast enough. "I
appreciate your time, but I have to go now." The last thing I
remember is leaving a ten-dollar co-pay on the counter and bolt-
ing out his office door.

As for my penis, it soon returned to normal, and by "normal"
I mean perfect. And that spot, I remember it fondly. Maybe I'm
even a little proud of it. I mean, it's not every penis that can be a
textbook model. Twice.

STOCKHOLM SYNDROME

For a brief period in 2015, I toyed with the idea of cashing in my chips and moving to Sweden, mostly because I had started to develop disturbing visions and convinced myself I could escape them by relocating to Scandinavia. Damon agreed to come along for the ride; he had been wanting to try authentic Swedish meatballs anyway.

I guess you could say my visions were religious in nature, even though I am not what most religious people would call religious. I believe there's a strong possibility that God exists. But I also believe there's an equally strong possibility that God is a concept humans created because we didn't understand things like gravity and lightning and DNA, and that we perpetuate because the thought of being one tiny speck out of billions of tiny specks on a large spherical mass orbiting a huge ball of fire, which is just one of immeasurable balls of fire out there in a pitch-black sky, is scary as fuck. And quite frankly, I don't understand how anyone who has given the topic considerable, rational thought can be 100 percent certain either way. But that's not important right now.

What's important is my vision. I didn't see Jesus in a waterfall or Buddha on an English muffin. One Sunday morning in the media room of our house in Connecticut I was watching *This Week with George Stephanopoulos* and witnessed something terrifying. It was Ted Cruz's face. No, his whole head actually. Words were coming out of it, like a normal head on a talk show, but then it turned bright red, swelled to twice its size, collapsed in on itself, and morphed into something resembling a prolapsed anus. You can imagine the horror. One minute Ted Cruz was a US senator and presidential hopeful; the next a pulsating, crimson, gurgling sphincter. And George didn't even bat an eye! That's how I know God was letting me, and only me, in on a pretty substantial secret.

I went upstairs to the kitchen, where Damon was making poached eggs.

"Good timing," he said. "These are almost done. Can you put the silverware on the table?"

"Sure," I said and grabbed two forks and knives.

"Is everything all right?" he asked. "You have a weird look on your face."

"Really? How so?"

"You look like you just smelled something really bad and can't figure out where it's coming from," he said. "Remember that time we found the dead mouse in the sofa?"

"Yeah, that was gross."

"Well, that's your face."

Over breakfast, I relayed what I saw, and Damon asked me how I knew what a prolapsed anus looked like. And so I had to explain how I had stumbled upon some photos of them a year or so ago during an innocent Google search. Well, maybe not completely innocent. I had been looking for images of Jon Hamm in tight pants.

"Wait," Damon said. "Why were you searching for pictures of Jon Hamm in tight pants?"

"I was curious about the Hammaconda, obvi. But will you please let me finish?" You see, I continued, Jon Hamm stars in *Mad Men*, which is about an ad agency in the sixties, and Darren from *Bewitched* also worked at an ad agency in the sixties, and Darren was constantly derided by his mother-in-law, Endora, played by Agnes Moorehead, who made her on-camera acting debut in *Citizen Kane* as the mother of Charles Foster Kane, who died thinking about his childhood sled named Rosebud. And if you type "Rosebud" into the search bar, you'll quickly learn it's the slang term for an inside-out anal sphincter. And if you're even slightly curious to see what one of those looks like, you will stumble upon images you can never fully expunge from your brain. Could happen to anyone, really.

The Ted Cruz visions continued and intensified as primary season approached, whipping me into a state of emotional distress. Every time I would turn on the news or engage in social media, there it was: the Satanic Rosebud, throbbing, pulsating, taunting and mocking me, threatening to swallow this great nation down its thorny gullet into a stinking pit of venomous bile. God was obviously speaking directly to me, but I wasn't sure why. Maybe it was a sign, I figured, a sign to get as far away as possible. So I booked us a weeklong trip to Stockholm, reasoning that if Cruz were elected president of the United States, we could move there for four or—heaven forbid—eight years. No big deal. On paper Sweden seemed like the perfect place for us. Its people, for the most part, speak English, are immaculately clean, and appreciate a cute outfit from H&M. That's pretty much me in a nutshell. We would go in mid-June for the summer solstice, I decided. Nineteen hours of sunlight!

On the flight over, Damon flipped through a Stockholm guidebook he had ordered online, pausing occasionally to ask me to remind him again why we might be moving to Sweden.

"Because Ted Cruz is the devil," I said.

"You've mentioned that a few dozen times," he replied. It was true. "But why can't we live in Paris? We love Paris. And you've been wanting to brush up on your French."

He was right. My French was very rusty, and I had been talking about enrolling in a two-week French immersion course in the south of France. But to be honest, the thought of actually going through with it gave me a migraine. "I'm getting too old to be fluent," I said. "The best time to learn a language is during your formative years. I've been fully formed for a while now. At this point I'm well into the decay phase."

"Okay," Damon said. "How about Sydney? We love Sydney and you've been talking about surfing more."

He was also right about that. The first time I tried surfing, in Hawaii, I turned out to be a little bit of a natural. I stood up on the board on my first attempt, rode a decent-sized wave, and impressed the hell out of my instructor. But to tell you the truth, I wasn't too surprised. I had been passively training for twenty years on mass transit. If I can't get a seat on the New York City subway, I stand, like everyone else. But I don't like touching the pole with my bare hands because, well, cooties. So, I'll just sort of stand there with my legs bent and my core engaged, and occasionally flail around like one of those inflatable air dancer things they have outside car washes.

But as much as I would like to hang ten with a bunch of tanned, six-packed Aussies, we couldn't move to Sydney because of Mary. "The dog, Damon, the dog," I said. "Australia requires a six-month pet quarantine. Didn't you even hear what happened to Johnny Depp?" (I was certain he had not.) "Over my dead body will Mary spend half a year in a kennel without me. *I'll* sleep in the goddamn kennel before I let that happen. I've already looked it up: we can get a dog passport for Sweden. She just needs a few shots."

We played this game for a solid hour, and I call it a game because neither of us really had any intention of leaving our family, friends, and careers in the United States. It's just nice to consider one's options.

Stockholm's Arlanda Airport is large and bright, with many windows overlooking the verdant landscape nearby. The polished dark hardwood floors, very similar to the ones we have in our house, shine in the natural light. "Look at the sheen on these," I remarked. "As you well know, these floors aren't as low-maintenance as they look. They seem like an unwise choice for a high-traffic area if you ask me." But Damon pointed out the near-complete absence of foot traffic. The people exiting our flight were the only people in the whole airport. Suddenly I was struck by the feeling of what it might be like to survive a zombie apocalypse.

I imagined a sequel to *The Walking Dead*: It's been ten years since the last zombie kicked the bucket, for the second time. A small group of Swedes and a highly sophisticated, well-dressed, middle-aged American man, played by me, of course, must reestablish civilization and procreate to repopulate the world. (My character and an adorable twentysomething lesbian, played by Jennifer Lawrence, reproduce via IVF.) Their first task is to clean shit up. They break out the Windex and the Pine Sol and just *go to town* for, like, the first three episodes, scrubbing, polishing, disinfecting . . .

"Look, ABBA," Damon said, interrupting my creative flow. He pointed to a life-sized cardboard cutout of the most famous singing group in Scandinavian history. I assumed it was an enlarged album cover from the 1970s, or maybe they still dressed in clingy bell-bottoms. I'm not so up-to-date on my ABBA news. "The one on the left's got quite the ABBAconda," I said.

Within one hour of settling into Stockholm—taking a taxi from the airport, checking in to our hotel, unpacking—we realized we were going to be bored to death for a week. Don't get me wrong, it's a fine city, pretty enough with lots of old, square buildings. And the food was surprisingly good. We discovered a love of *skagen*, basically a shrimp salad on toast, and found a place that served the most amazing Swedish meatballs, which I consumed greedily, despite the fact that they contained veal. (I co-organized The Anti-Veal-Eaters Revolt in the eighth grade and never really looked back.) And the fine citizens of Stockholm are excruciatingly civilized, if slightly depressed and—I got the impression—slightly insecure about their city. Practically every local we met asked our opinion of the place.

"How do you like it here?" a salesman in a clothing store asked Damon while I was trying on a sweater.

"The sun is up for a really long time," Damon replied, and the salesman nodded in resigned agreement.

We took a ferry ride and a nice old man asked us how long we were staying in town. A week, we said.

"Too long," he responded. "I was born here, but forty years ago I moved to Sydney."

"We have a dog," I said. "We can't do that." The old guy looked at me as though something had been lost in translation. It hadn't. I'm just incapable of rational thought around the subject of my dog.

We mostly just walked around quoting *Trading Places*, one of our favorite movies.

"I am Inga from Sveden."

"But you're wearing lederhosen."

"Ya, for sure, from Sveden. Please to help me with my rucksack?"

On the third day, we decided to visit the Vasa Museum, the main attraction of which is an elaborately decorated seventeenth-century warship, the *Vasa*, that was so poorly engineered that it went ass over tea kettle and sank on its maiden voyage, right in the center of Stockholm Harbor. Three hundred years later, it was salvaged, reconstructed, and preserved in the museum, a feat Swedes seem very proud of. The museum, or *museet*, is actually a pretty enjoyable way to spend an hour and a half out of nineteen excruciatingly long hours of daylight.

Exhibitions throughout the *museet* have been designed to give you a taste of what life aboard the ship might have been like. For example, for 450 passengers, the vast majority being soldiers and sailors, there was one dentist, who was responsible for everything from tooth extractions to limb amputations. If a sailor was disrespectful to the admiral, he could be keelhauled. That's when they tie you to a rope, throw you off one side of the ship and pull you out the other side, dragging you under the keel of the boat. In the middle of the ocean. For being disrespectful.

"Hey, Admiral, your father's meatballs are huge and salty."

"Under the boat with you, Sven!"

"What? I grew up next door to you. He's a really good cook!"

And maybe even more incomprehensible: two toilets. For 450 men spending their days drinking beer and eating nonrefrigerated meat! Can you even imagine the line for those things after a meal of half-rotten caribou kebabs? I can't. I'm the kind of guy who gags on an airplane when someone two rows ahead of me farts in his sleep.

Divers also recovered several skeletons of people who got trapped aboard the ship as it sank, some of whom were women. (Historians aren't even sure what women were doing aboard the ship in the first place.) Based on mineral testing and X-rays of the bones, scientists determined that pretty much everyone had suffered from severe malnutrition as a child or walked with a limp because of injuries that had never healed properly.

In the darkest part of the *museet*, six heads glow from inside glass cases. They're creations of forensic artists, facial reconstructions of six skulls found in the muddy wreckage. There's a blatant honesty and exactness you might expect from a Swedish forensic artist, from the enlarged pores they added to broken capillaries to overgrown eyebrow hair. If this ship had sunk off the coast of, say, Barcelona, I'm sure the reconstruction would have gone much differently. All the dead people would look like Calvin Klein fragrance models on the receiving end of fellatio. But not these old Swedes. They are rough-and-tumble.

Except Beata, whose reconstructed face caught my eye. She was beautiful, in that profoundly dejected kind of way. Physically she was a mix of weak and strong features: pronounced cheekbones and a big nose that appeared to have been broken once or twice, small blue eyes, thin lips, and a ruddy complexion. Her blond hair was pulled back from her face, covered by something resembling a folded dish towel. I've done so many makeovers in my life that I'm almost embarrassed to admit my first thought was, *With a little concealer and the right lipstick, I could make this chick look like Uma Thurman.*

But I let that moment pass. I looked at Beata for a while, and she looked at me. Her expression was that of a woman who had been thoroughly beaten down. What were you doing aboard this ship full of men, Beata? I wondered. Were you a stowaway? Were you a whore? Was it your job to clean those two toilets? Was life so bad on land that the sea seemed like an escape? An adventure? And who broke your nose? Some guy you were shacking up with? Your father? Your mother?

I just could not even fathom a situation in which this woman's life was anything but pure misery. Only thirty or so people died aboard the *Vasa*. Because it had barely left the dock, most passengers just swam to safety. But why did Beata die? Maybe she got pinned under a table or crate when the boat capsized. Or maybe she couldn't swim. Or maybe going down with the ship was better than going back to shore.

Tell me, Beata. Tell me!

"Hey handsome." Damon had walked up behind me. He whispered in my ear, "What are you thinking?"

"Oh, you know, just the usual nonsense," I said. "How do you feel about picking up and going to Paris tomorrow?"

"I think that is a brilliant idea."

The Internet service in Sweden is pretty fast, so we were able to book a flight to Paris and a hotel room in the First Arrondissement in less than fifteen minutes. It's not that Sweden is unlovable, or unlivable, it just wasn't our cup of glögg.

Paris, on the other hand, can make you feel like all is right with the world, that every cathedral deserves flying buttresses, every meal deserves dessert, and every pedestrian deserves painful but gorgeous shoes.

Damon and I were walking through the immaculately groomed gardens of the Tuileries when our phones started to blow up. It was June 26, 2015, and the US Supreme Court had just ruled that same-sex couples were entitled to all the benefits of marriage on a federal level. We both teared up. Our lives are nothing short of amazing, filled with people we love and who love us, but sometimes you don't realize you've been a second-class citizen until you've received the right to be first-class.

We decided that to celebrate I should post our wedding picture on my Facebook fan page. It's a candid shot of us taken in our backyard in Connecticut. We're holding hands as we walk down the stone steps to our pond, where our friends and family were waiting for us. Neither of us is looking into the camera but we're beaming with joy.

The post received 180,000 "likes" and more than 6,000 people stopped whatever they were doing that day to wish us love and congratulations.

Five people thought it was appropriate to tell us we were going to hell.

If you've never been told by a complete stranger that you're going to hell, let me try to explain the feeling to you. It makes you feel something like sadness, but it's not quite sadness. Sadness is when your favorite grandfather dies or your parents tell you the dog you grew up with has cancer. And it's not really anger, because anger is when you see a drunk driver on the highway in front of you when you've got your family in the car. And it's not exactly pity, because pity is what you feel when you pass a homeless mother and her two children on the street. It's all of those emotions rolled up into one not-yet-named-in-English emotion. But it doesn't consume you in the fiery way that rage can or the chest-crushing way sorrow can. It's smaller, subtler, like a thousand shallow pinpricks.

Soon after the marriage equality ruling, Ted Cruz called the day "some of the darkest twenty-four hours in our nation's history." And at that moment I realized why I had been having disturbing visions of his face: God wanted me to know, in no uncertain terms, that Ted Cruz is a huge, painful asshole.

And that even if he, or someone just as horrible, becomes president, it's not worth jumping ship.

THE WAY IT WENT

Clayton,* recently hired as a host for what would prove to be a short-lived home shopping network aimed at an upwardly mobile audience, sat at his desk writing notes on his blue cards for the next day's show. He had never been good at sitting still for any extended period of time, so his gaze frequently strayed to the plain-faced clock on the wall nearby. It was 4:50 p.m., so he could leave the office unnoticed in a little more than an hour. He had to prepare for a date that night with Tim, a handsome computer programmer with curly black hair he had met at the gym four months earlier.

The casual nature of his relationship with Tim made Clayton anxious. Clayton preferred clearly defined classifications when it came to men he was romantically involved with because they helped manage all parties' expectations, especially his own. For example, "dating" meant going on dates. Guys who were "going steady" were sexually monogamous. If you were "fuck buddies," you had regular sex without dinner or emotional commitment. And "boyfriends"

---

* All names have been changed, including my own.

were two guys working toward a common goal, like eventually sharing an apartment or adopting a dog. (Where Clayton acquired these definitions, he did not know, yet he regarded them as absolutes. Such is the wisdom of a twenty-five-year-old.)

Clayton/Tim fit into none of these categories. They went on dates that led to sex, of course, but they never talked of a future past Friday or Saturday night, so it seemed to Clayton that they were "dating." But recently their individual friend clusters had intertwined so that the two groups now attended the same parties, which suggested to Clayton a certain deepening of commitment. Tim had even let Clayton's friend Fiona hold his penis once as he peed during a party at a stranger's apartment on the Lower East Side. An intimate act if ever there was one! Granted, Clayton was perplexed as to why a straight woman would want to hold a gay man's penis— let alone *any* penis—during urination. And why a gay man would agree to it. And how the hell the topic came up in the first place.

A girl from the office stopped by Clayton's desk and sat on it, which he found odd. The typical work friend might lean on a colleague's desk, he thought, or stand there unassisted, honoring the concept of personal space. But he didn't even know her name, just her face, and that was because she sat along the route to the men's room.

"Hi, I'm Isabel," she said.

"Hi," he replied. "I'm Clayton."

"I know that, silly. You're a host. Everyone who works here knows your name." She had shoulder-length dark blond hair, which was neither sophisticated nor sassy, yet she somehow managed to project that she considered herself both. "So . . . I'm pretty new to town and I don't really know anyone. Do you want to hang out tomorrow night?"

"Sure," Clayton said, because he couldn't think of anything else to say and because he kind of felt sorry for her. New York can be the loneliest place on earth if you're not careful. It's surprisingly easy to be overlooked by 8 million people, he had discovered quickly, lest you remind them of your existence on a near-constant basis.

"Great," she said, dropping a tightly folded piece of steno paper near his keyboard. She hopped down from the desk and strode away, as suddenly as she had arrived.

As Clayton unfolded the paper, which contained Isabel's phone number as well as her address, he began to feel angry at the way he had been ambushed. That's not how Saturday night plans were made! You didn't make Saturday night plans until Saturday afternoon. That was the way it worked in New York. At about 3 p.m. on Saturday, you would call a few friends and set an agenda for the evening that could be amended or canceled at will depending on better offers that may or may not arise. But now he *had* plans, which interfered with his *lack* of plans, and made Clayton feel very *un*cool just as he had been beginning to feel *sort of* cool.

Once home, Clayton showered and groomed and changed into a fresh pair of khakis and the light-blue button-front linen shirt he had bought at Banana Republic for the occasion. Around seven Tim called and suggested they meet for dinner at a small restaurant near his apartment in Chelsea at eight. Clayton took two subways to get there and arrived looking more rumpled than he would have preferred. They had martinis and spoke about their jobs, their friends, and recent parties they thought were either lame or amazing. They also talked about spaetzle. Clayton, who had never heard of it, read it aloud from the menu as *spahtz-el.*

"It's *shpets-luh,*" Tim said.

"Oh," said Clayton. "Well, now I feel stupid. Should I have known that?"

"It's like an Eastern European pasta," Tim said. "You should order it. You know, expand your horizons a little." He smiled and looked down at his menu.

Clayton didn't know if Tim was mocking him or being sincere. Though Tim was a few years older, he seemed considerably more worldly. Clayton ordered the spaetzle, which was good, if a little bland. Little did he know at the time he wouldn't eat it again for another fifteen years, not because he didn't like it, but because the occasion rarely seemed to present itself. They split the check, and Tim asked Clayton if he'd like to come back to his apartment.

"Sure."

They walked to Tim's apartment, immediately undressed and began to have sex (the details of which will be left to the reader's imagination). About seven minutes in, Tim stopped all movement and said rather matter-of-factly, "I've got something to tell you."

Clayton froze. "OK," he said. This, stopping sex once it had begun, was highly unusual. He wondered if Tim was about to ask him to go steady.

They sat next to each other on the bed and didn't bother to cover themselves, even though the lights were on, because they were young. "You know how I took a business trip to London last week . . ." Tim began.

"Yes . . ." Clayton said. He had seen Tim the night before he left. Clayton had thought that was nice, making a point to see him for dinner and sex before leaving town.

"Well, while I was there, I had a threeway."

Threeway, thought Clayton, *that means two other people were involved.* Were they both men? British men? Or other Americans on business trips? Were they a man and a woman? (Tim had let Fiona hold his penis!) Probably both men, he decided, but were they better-looking than himself? Because if they were better-looking—square-jawed, polo-playing Eton types—he would feel very insecure about his own looks—and naked body—right now. But if they were not as good-looking—malnourished, bald chain-smokers—he would be turned off by Tim because that would mean that Tim was the type of guy who had sex with ugly people, which would mean that Clayton was ugly because they had been having sex until just a minute ago!

Clayton decided that asking too many questions would not be playing it cool, so he said, "That's cool."

"You don't care?" asked Tim.

"Why would I? We're not going steady or anything."

Tim cocked his head and furrowed his brow. "Do people say 'going steady' anymore?" he asked.

"You know what I mean. Being exclusive."

Apparently relieved that his disclosure had been met with such nonchalance, Tim began to kiss Clayton on the neck. Clayton lay motionless, images of uncircumsized English wangs and crooked teeth flooding his brain. "I'm not in the mood anymore, so I'm gonna head home," he said.

Clayton was hoping Tim would object to that notion, at least a bit. But he didn't. "OK," said Tim.

Clayton got up from the bed, picked up his clothes from the floor, and began to get dressed. His linen shirt was severely wrinkled and he didn't need to look in a mirror to know that his hair was a mess. He hated so much that he looked disheveled precisely when he wanted to appear smooth. Tim got out of bed, removed a cigarette from its pack, and lit it. When Clayton had buttoned his last button, Tim, still naked and semierect, opened the door to the hallway.

"I'm really not sure why you decided to tell me that during sex," Clayton said on his way out.

"I was just trying to be honest with you," Tim said.

Clayton gave Tim a peck on the lips. "Well, you shouldn't have," he said and squeezed Tim's penis, just slightly harder than might be comfortable.

The next morning Clayton awoke wondering whether Tim had gone out to a party, or, more likely, parties, after his exit, and if so, whether he and his friends shared a laugh over Clayton's prudishness. *He stormed out after I told him I had a threeway*, he could imagine Tim saying. *Oh, my God, what a girl*, his friends would laugh, even Fiona if she were there. Clayton began to doubt whether he was cut out for the complexities of gay life in New York, a feeling exacerbated by the fact that he was still sharing a tiny one-bedroom apartment with his ex-boyfriend, Pete, whom he could hear making breakfast in the kitchen three feet away.

After their breakup, Pete had moved the queen-sized bed, which was his, into the living room, and Clayton moved the futon, the only piece of furniture he owned, into the bedroom. Ever since, a sepia-toned haze of disappointment filled the apartment. Their relationship had failed (disappointment in each other) but neither could afford to move out (disappointment in themselves).

Clayton had met Pete while attending grad school and waiting tables on weekends. Pete came to the restaurant occasionally with friends who were regulars. "Pete wants to ask you out on a date," said Pete's friend one night when he was sans Pete. "Then Pete should ask me out on a date," Clayton answered. And the next night Pete stopped into the bar to have a drink.

"Your friend says you want to ask me out," said Clayton while waiting for the bartender to mix the drinks for his four-top.

"Yeah, he's been saying I should go out more."

Pete was very handsome with sharp features and a toothy smile, and Clayton wondered why he was so bashful.

"If you asked me out, I'd say yes," said Clayton.

"Do you want to go out with me?" asked Pete.

Clayton picked up his cocktail tray. "Not really." Pete looked stricken. "I'm teasing. Of course I do. You're adorable."

Their relationship got serious quickly. When Clayton finished his course work, he applied for jobs locally but received no offers, and so he moved back home to Long Island with his parents and began to answer want ads in the *New York Times*, which eventually led to a job as an assistant editor at a small trade magazine reporting on the electronics industry. Pete said he was ready to move to New York, and the two found the apartment they now shared. The problem was that Clayton's vision of Manhattan life involved a whirlwind of throbbing nightclubs, fancy restaurants, and designer clothes. Pete wanted to cook chicken and watch television, like they'd done back in grad school. But grad school is not having a real job. And it wasn't long before Clayton cheated on Pete with a wealthy executive of a design firm. They remained civil after their breakup, however, friendly even. But they eventually lost touch.

Clayton went to work and sold some inline skates and protective gear. Saturdays were supposed to be busy ones in the home shopping world, but sales at the new channel were low. Nobody seemed to really care. "We're finding our feet," executives would say, and Clayton believed them. Around five that evening he reluctantly called Isabel and asked what she wanted to do. When she said she didn't know, Clayton suggested they take a walk around Soho and find a bar. Isabel asked if Clayton would pick her up at her apartment in Hell's Kitchen. He found the request an imposition, but she probably didn't realize he lived on the Upper East Side. Anyone who has lived in Manhattan for more than five minutes knows that asking someone to travel crosstown for your own convenience is akin to requesting a loan, or a kidney.

After an excruciating ride on the bus, Clayton rang the buzzer to Isabel's apartment and she came downstairs a few minutes later wearing a baggy shift dress and flat sandals. Because of its lack of shape and large yellow floral print, the dress seemed to him something a mother of three would wear to a daytime wedding near the beach. She must have noticed the look of consternation on his face because she announced quite loudly on Tenth Avenue, "I've gained so much weight that I've resorted to wearing *frocks*!"

Something about the way she said frocks struck him as vulgar—and to be speaking so loudly about one's weight in public. Granted, she was about five feet tall and a size 8, a bit plumper than most women her age living in Manhattan in 1994. He wanted so much to go home, to go anywhere actually, to relieve himself of this obligation. But he had committed himself to showing her around town. He could feign a headache or emergency, but she would be able to detect the lie, wouldn't she? Then she would go back to her apartment, feeling rejected and alone. He couldn't do that to her.

As they walked and made small talk about her neighborhood (noisy!) and the weather (hot!), they found themselves at a subway entrance. Clayton suggested they take it downtown, but Isabel protested. "No!" she exclaimed. "I can't ride the *sub*way."

Assuming she was afraid, he tried to assuage her fear. "It's really not so bad," he said, "especially at this time of day."

"No. It just won't do. We'll take a taxi. I'll pay." He reluctantly obliged, though it would take twice as long, which meant he would have to engage in more conversation without the benefit of alcohol or the distraction of strangers.

Once in Soho, they settled on a large bar offering flights of wine: six small glasses per order, served on paper placemats printed with boxes in which one could jot down notes like "citrusy" or "oaky" or "hints of quince." They discussed their respective bosses. Hers was a family friend who'd needed an executive assistant, while his was a *nouveau riche* type he nicknamed The Gucc (pronounced "gooch") because of her apparent uniform of Gucci loafers. Clayton decided after two flights of wine each that Isabel was not so terrible, but around eleven o'clock he suggested they call it a night; he didn't know of any parties and wasn't sure he wanted to bring her to one anyway. Then Isabel asked, "Do you have a girlfriend?"

He found the question absurd. "God, no," he said with a nervous laugh.

"So . . . do you have a boyfriend?"

This chick is ballsy, he thought. "Not at the moment," he said, "no."

"So, you're gay."

"I thought that was pretty obvious." Clayton signaled the bartender for the check.

"I'm not like most women," she said.

"How so?" he asked.

"I can just have sex and not expect anything else."

"Good for you." Clayton was starting to get very uncomfortable. He reached into his pocket and pulled out eighty dollars. "I think that should cover it."

"Do you want to have sex with me?" she asked.

He thought about it for a moment. "Not really."

"Have you ever had sex with a woman before?"

"Sort of, almost, in high school," he said. "But my parents interrupted—they came home from a party early—and I just figured, eh, it wasn't meant to be."

"But aren't you curious?"

Clayton had been asked this question about one hundred times since coming out of the closet. He was curious about a lot of stuff, he would say, like whether drowning was a painless way to die or if he could outrun a raccoon should the need arise, but that didn't mean he wanted to do any of those things. "Not really," he told Isabel. "I have to work in the morning, so I think we should go."

They left the bar, and Clayton hailed a cab. When it pulled up to the curb in front of them, he opened the door for Isabel and kissed her on the cheek, the way one would say good-bye to a new friend. "Aren't you getting in?" she asked.

He explained that he would take the 6 train from Spring Street.

"Oh, come on, share a cab with me," she said. "I'll pay."

She hadn't even offered to split the bar tab, so he decided to take her up on the offer. He climbed into the taxi and closed the door behind him. "We'll be making two stops," he told the driver. "One on Sixty-First and First and then over on Fifty-Fifth and Tenth."

Before they had even crossed Houston Street, though, Isabel had wriggled out of her panties, straddled him, and stuck her tongue in Clayton's mouth. "Oh, fuck it," he told the cab driver, "just make one stop on Fifty-Fifth and Tenth." He couldn't turn down such a direct offer of sex, from a woman no less! She must have sensed something in him, which he had not sensed in himself. Maybe some kind of pheromone.

As he followed the giant-flowered frock up three flights of stairs to its owner's apartment, Clayton wondered at how he had gotten himself into this situation—and how he could get out of it. Was he really going to have sex with a member of the opposite sex, just because she was expecting it? Or was that what she was expecting at all? Maybe she just wanted to make out for a while, he told himself. He did that all the time in college. But why would she remove her panties?

"There's a condom on the nightstand," she said. "I'm going into the bathroom. Have it on when I come out."

"Sure," he said.

They had sex (the details of which will be left to the reader's imagination) and when it was over, Clayton said, "I guess I'll get going now."

"No," she said. "You have to stay over."

"I do?" He was confused.

"That's the way it goes."

He supposed it was the gentlemanly thing to do. Plus, he didn't want her to think he was running away like some completely flustered gay guy, which he absolutely was. So he got back into her bed and stared up at the ceiling for approximately six hours. He had barely fallen asleep when she initiated sex again (the details of which will be left to the reader's imagination).

She got out of bed and put on a red kimono-style robe. "You have to take me to breakfast now. That's the way it goes."

They sat across from each other at a nearby diner. She ordered a spinach and feta omelet with a side of bacon, toast, and home fries, all of which she devoured as though she had spent the last month in a Turkish prison. He ordered pancakes, which he pushed away from him after two bites.

After breakfast, Clayton reminded Isabel that even though it was Sunday, he had to work, the glamorous life of a home-shopping host being what it was. She thanked him for breakfast—he had paid for that too—and said she hoped they could hang out again some time. He said sure.

Clayton walked east across Seventy-Second Street until he reached Central Park, where a steady stream of joggers and bicyclists were headed south in their great counterclockwise loop. He crossed through them when given the opportunity and into Sheep Meadow. Though it was empty now, later in the day this well-manicured lawn would be packed with people his age who couldn't afford a vacation house in the Hamptons, Fire Island, or the Jersey Shore. He knew this because he was one of them. He was less than halfway across the lawn when he decided he couldn't bear the thought of his polo shirt touching his body—perhaps it was the humidity of this August morning—so he took it off and held it limply by his side. He wanted so much to lie down on the grass but he knew he might fall asleep there, probably for too long. He considered the embarrassment of being discovered by an acquaintance who had come to the park to get some sun and be flirty with guys on other blankets and continued his trek.

When Clayton arrived at his building, he put his shirt back on, feeling sufficiently like a degenerate. He unlocked his apartment door to find Pete, standing in the hallway wearing pajama bottoms and no shirt, sipping coffee from an oversized mug, which looked particularly large because of Pete's small body. "Looks like someone had a fun night," Pete said.

"I don't know if I'd say that, but it was a night."

Pete offered Clayton coffee, which he accepted, and while he was pouring it from the carafe, he asked, "What time do you go to work?"

"I have to be there at one," Clayton said. "So I'll leave around twelve thirty. Why?"

"I was wondering if you wanted to have sex." Pete smiled. He had big, perfect teeth, which Clayton envied. "I've never even had braces," he had told Clayton on their first date.

"Sure," said Clayton. "Why the hell not."

So Pete and Clayton had sex (the details of which will be left to the reader's imagination). When it was over, Clayton ran the shower and when the temperature was to his liking, entered the tub and sat down, his head resting on the back wall. He stayed like that for more than half an hour, until Pete knocked on the bathroom door to remind him to go to work.

On Monday morning Clayton went to the office for meetings with buyers and executives. Around lunchtime while he was checking his sales figures on his computer, Isabel plopped onto his desk again. Her legs were crossed at the ankles and her hands clasped along the edge on either side of her knees, the way a schoolgirl might sit while waiting her turn in a spelling bee.

She looked around for witnesses and, seeing none, said at a conversational volume, "So that was fun." When Clayton responded with an *mmm hmmm* and an obvious lack of eye contact, Isabel dropped her head closer to his. "I could have you fired, you know," she said. Her tone seemed remarkably upbeat and flirty.

Clayton, too tired for games, looked Isabel in the eye and said, "Actually, I don't think you could." And he went back to his computer screen.

Some small part of Clayton wondered whether Isabel would tell her boss the truth, a fiction, or anything at all. But as the days went by his concern diminished steadily. Soon the channel laid off almost half its employees, including Isabel.

Eight years later, Clayton was walking in the West Village one evening with his boyfriend, Alex, and someone—Isabel!— grabbed his arm. "How *are* you?" she asked warmly, as if address- ing a best friend she hadn't seen in years.

It took him a second to place her; to be honest he couldn't remember her name immediately. "I'm good, thank you," he said. "You?"

"I'm . . . great," she said. "Yeah, I'm great."

And that was it. They said good-bye. A few steps later, Alex asked, "Who was that?"

"Just some girl I used to work with," Clayton said. "Do you want to go back to your place and have sex?"

"Sure," said Alex.

(And the details of which—oh, you get the idea.)

I'M WAITING

I haven't waited a table since March 1993, but I still wake up in a cold sweat a couple of times a year because I forgot to bring a third whiskey sour to the naked old lady dining with Idi Amin. Or because the management has changed the computer system without telling me, so every time I type the code for a menu item it gets all garbled by the time it reaches the printer in the kitchen.

"Is this some kind of joke, you little prick?" The expediting chef screams at me as soon as I enter through the swinging doors.

I'm confused. "Is what a joke?" I ask.

"What did you order?" He looks like he wants to rip my head off.

"A turkey club, hold the mayonnaise."

"Look at this!" He thrusts the ticket toward me. It's got my name on the top, so it must be my order except, for the life of me, I don't know why it doesn't say TURK CLB, NO MAYO. "Read it out loud," he says, "so these fine chefs don't miss a single word." A half-dozen surly types in white coats glare at me.

"Ass rape, no mayo," I say.

"Louder, boy!"

"ASS RAPE, NO MAYO, SIR!"

Then the chef—he has become Brad Pitt in *Inglourious Basterds*—paces back and forth in front of the steam table where they keep the soups: Manhattan Clam, New England Clam, and whatever the soup du jour is. I probably should know it, but I forgot to memorize the specials. "Did ya hear that, fellas? This fine sonofabitch wants nonconsensual sodomy! With a categorical lack of lubricant!"

All of a sudden I'm confused because I don't know how my customer is going to get his sandwich. "No," I say. "That's not what I want at all. Nobody wants that. Can somebody please make me a turkey club?" The next thing I know, I'm running and running. I'm the only waiter for the entire restaurant. All the water glasses need to be refilled, ashtrays are overflowing, my name tag says Charlene.

"Noooooooo!" I sit up in bed.

"Are you OK?" Damon asks.

"Just another restaurant dream," I say and try to go back to sleep.

If I ever become president of the United States, which I won't because I want that job about as much as I want bacterial meningitis, I vow to institute a draft. Not for military service, but for mandatory restaurant work, which will result in a more kindhearted society overall.

Hear me out.

I will require every citizen over the age of twenty-one to wait tables *full-time* for a *minimum* of two years. You might get drafted on your twenty-first birthday. Maybe on your forty-seventh. Perhaps when you're eighty-two. Nobody knows, because it's random. When you receive via certified mail the notice that you have been drafted, you will report immediately to the Bureau of Food and Beverage Service where you will be given an apron and some soft-soled shoes with decent arch support. Then you will be randomly assigned to a restaurant within a fifteen-mile radius of your home, to make fulfilling your service requirement as convenient as possible.

A wealthy, frozen-faced housewife might find herself slinging bowls of pho during the lunch rush at Saigon Sally's on Route 6. The newest cocktail server at the Bellagio hotel and casino: a balding insurance salesman named Herb. Can't find grandma? That's because for the third time this week she picked up an extra shift at Hooters.

Just to be clear, the point of my program is not to level the economic playing field. This country is too far gone to fix that mess. I just think it's important each of us experience the utter assholery of which our fellow American is capable while he's eating a pork chop. If we're all concerned that tomorrow we may be the one treated like the lowly pissant, smiling like a lunatic for a 15 percent tip, we will all behave more civilly today.

While in graduate school, I took a job in a relatively small restaurant in Chicago's Lakeview East neighborhood, which is also known as Boystown because of the high percentage of gay men living there. And though the restaurant wasn't a gay one per se, a lot, maybe half, of the clientele preferred members of the same sex. Inside, eighteen tables, all deuces and four-tops, were arranged in an L shape around an old wooden bar. The food was American, with an Italian spin, insomuch as there was roasted garlic on the appetizer menu and olive oil on every table. If the weather was nice, the manager would have the waiters, never more than three (plus a bartender), uncover from beneath a tarpaulin six more tables outside on the sidewalk. The place could have used a busboy, but for whatever reason none was employed, which meant that the waiters had to do all the clearing, scraping, resetting, dropping bread, and refilling water in addition to taking food and drink orders and delivering them. I didn't mind the work, and no bussers meant more cash in my pocket. But when it was busy, an extra set of hands would have been helpful, especially with all the tables in my station full at once.

Waiting on gay guys can be a fun—or horrible—experience if you are one. Sometimes the manager would seat a table of men past their prime in my station because they were obviously more excited about flirting with their twenty-three-year-old waiter than they were about the food. "Does that steak come with a side of tall, skinny white boy?" they'd say. Or once: "I'll have a martini, and you make sure it's dirty. Dirty as that little mind of yours. Oh, that's right, I can see into your filthy soul, you wicked twink slut." It was adorable.

I'll tell you one thing, though: When a perverted old dude tells you his table is wobbly, don't get on your hands and knees to check the screws on the bottom of the table legs. Because when you spot those two enormous hairy balls hanging out of an open fly, you will hit your head on the underside of the table. Every. Time.

The worst kind of gay table is a four-top of perfectly manicured, well-dressed homosexuals in their late twenties. The *worst*. They're so predictable because they always follow this formula: one alpha, two betas, and a gamma. The alpha is the gorgeous one. He's got a head full of perfect hair, neon-white teeth, and a jawline so sharp you could use it to slice most semisoft cheeses. He's also got broad gym-puffed shoulders and a waist that looks tiny—even when he's sitting down. Then, there's the gamma, who through no fault of his own just wasn't genetically blessed. Maybe the gamma's eyes are a little too bulgy or he has a weak chin, you know, the kind of stuff you can't fix without really expensive surgery and even if you do, you end up looking worse. Those two are easy to deal with.

The alpha's self-possessed because he spends his life with people gawking at him. It's like waiting on the Queen of England. "I'll have the fish." Across the table, the gamma knows he'll never be the object of anyone's lustful attention, at least not in this crowd, so he resigns himself to being the affable one. Someone has to do it because the two betas surely won't. They're handsome too, but unlike the alpha, they're not traffic-stopping beauties. One beta might have really thin lips, the other a too-upturned nose. Well aware of their (some would say minor) flaws, they secretly despise the alpha for being so exquisite. And all this bitterness has to be released somewhere, so the gay waiter is the perfect receptacle.

And it's not that they're obnoxious; overt rudeness would tip off the others, including the server, to a simmering resentment. It's a look up and down the waiter's uniform. A questioning of the waiter's aural faculties. ("I said sauce on the side. You heard that, right?") A blank stare when asked if the food was cooked to their liking. Oh, the gays. Having been both a beta and a gamma, depending on the company, I can tell you, we've got so many issues. On the whole, the gays are good tippers though. Even when they've brought their date to the table on a leash.

Every spring the International Mr. Leather conference is held in Chicago and attended by thousands of gay men with leather fetishes, some of whom—I'm not sure of the percentage—are into BDSM. I'll just state for the record that at the time I knew nothing about the leather subculture, which is only slightly less than I know about it now. And I don't judge. I *do not care one iota* about what turns you or anyone else on sexually, as long as everyone involved is a consenting adult. And no animals at all. I mean, if you stick a gerbil up someone's ass or screw a horse, I hate you and you should go to jail. As far as I can tell, most leather men like to wear chaps and jeans or a leather codpiece, maybe a leather cuff or two and dance shirtless. Who cares. Knock yourself out. I'll be at home watching *Rear Window* for the umpteenth time. I just can't get enough of that Grace Kelly.

On this Saturday night, during leather weekend, two men in their late thirties arrived at Cornelia's for dinner. One wore tight black leather pants and a black leather jacket unzipped halfway to reveal a tanned chest covered in coarse dark hair. A vintage-looking motorcycle cap with an eagle medallion and a chain across the brim sat atop his head. His mustache was shaped like a horseshoe. Let's call him L.D. for Leather Daddy. His companion I'll call S.B. for Slave Boy. He was dressed similarly, though his leather pants were not as revealing in the crotch. He was shirtless under his jacket too, save for a studded black leather harness worn across the chest. His head was shaved, maybe four days earlier judging by the length of the stubble, and he wore a choker collar, about two inches wide, with a chain attached to it, the other end of which L.D. was holding in his right hand.

When the manager sat L.D. and S.B. by the window in my station, I said to him, "Wouldn't it be better if Thomas took that table?" Thomas, who pronounced his name *tow-MAS*, was a fellow waiter whose hair had a tendency to flop into his eyes when he was busy. His retro black-framed glasses made him look like a 1950s chemistry grad student, but he was actually working toward his doctorate in English. He had mentioned to me at the start of the shift that he had a date after work with some guy in town for the convention.

"You want me to ask them to *move*?" the manager asked.

"No, not move," I said. "Thomas could take them, and I'll take his next table."

"Are you *scared* of them or something?"

"No I'm not *scared* of them," I said. It was sort of a lie. "I just don't think they'll like me." In fact, I'm pretty sure the manager didn't like me very much ever since I corrected his pronunciation of *pollo*. There was a dish on the menu called *pollo alla pesto*, which was one of the more popular menu items at the restaurant and for good reason. It was farfalle pasta with chunks of chicken in a basil pesto sauce that contained golden raisins. Two decades later, I still make it, usually in the summer with fresh basil and grilled chicken. My version is delicious. Anyway, he was calling it *POY-o alla pesto*, and I said I was pretty sure it was *PO-lo alla pesto*, because the dish was Italian-inspired, not Spanish.

"Why are you in Chicago again?" he asked me.

"I'm getting my master's in journalism at Northwestern," I said.

"You're not studying restaurant management?"

"No."

"Then shut up."

He was kind of a dick.

He told me I couldn't trade tables with Thomas, out of spite, I was sure. I grabbed a water pitcher from the service station and approached my new deuce. "Hi, guys, my name is Clinton, I'll be your waiter tonight. Can I get—"

"Vodka and cranberry," said L.D. without looking up at me.

"—you something from the bar." I can't stand being inter-rupted. "One vodka and cranberry, and how about for you, sir?" I tried to make eye contact with S.B., who had that faraway look that models sometimes have, the kind that simultaneously conveys hunger, fatigue, and a general disgust of anything with a pulse.

"He'll have nothing," said L.D. "Take his water glass away."

"Okey doke." I grabbed the water glass and removed it from the table.

I went to the bar to order the vodka and cranberry from the bartender, an older, portly guy in his late fifties who had taken a liking to me from the start because I was from New York. He had spent some time there in the seventies and eighties, he said, sleeping around and doing a shit-ton of drugs. He didn't age too well because of it. He made it clear that Chicago had not been his first choice, but he had settled down with a nice guy and they had two small lap dogs.

"Can I get a Cape Codder for table ten, Robert?"

"Of course, my dear," he said. He had a deep, raspy voice but feminine mannerisms, which resulted in him seeming both fatherly and motherly. I found the juxtaposition soothing. "What's the daddy having?" I was confused and I must have looked it. He asked again: "I assume the sissy drink is for the bitch on the leash. What's daddy drinking?"

"The one on the leash isn't having anything. The vodka cran-berry is for the . . . master?"

A look of sheer repulsion came over his face. I was glad he had his back to them. "In my day," he said, "a leather daddy top wouldn't be caught *dead* drinking *punch*." He made the drink and pushed it across the service area to me. "Goddamn poseurs," he said. I put a lime wheel on the rim of the glass and added a swizzle stick because that's the way I had been taught to garnish a Cape Codder.

When I arrived back at the table, S.B. was looking out the window at nothing in particular and L.D. was examining his own fingernails.

"Here we go, one vodka and cran—"

"I didn't ask for lime." He removed the lime wheel and tossed it like a miniature Frisbee at S.B., who didn't even flinch. It hit his chest below the harness and landed in his lap.

"—berry. Okaayyyy." I worried that the acidic lime juice would stain S.B.'s leather pants. "Do you want me to take that from you?" I held out my palm to take the lime.

S.B. didn't answer. I was starting to get the feeling someone had taken a few too many downers before dinner.

"Angel hair with shrimp," L.D. said, handing me both menus.

"You got it," I replied. I assumed S.B. needed to eat too. He looked so hungry. "Can I get you anything?"

"Don't talk to him," snapped L.D. At this point, I was starting to get a little pissed off. I mean, I can talk to whomever the hell I want, especially if he's a full-grown man sitting in my station and it's my freakin' job to bring him food. Plus, I really don't like being told what to do, but I needed the job and didn't want to make a scene.

As I mentioned, leather really isn't my thing. And dominance and submission stuff has never really resonated with me either. It goes against what is probably my most fervent core value: fairness. Damon and I say things to each other like, "I'll choose the restaurant, you choose the movie," "I'll cut the sandwich in two, you choose which half you want," "I'll go down to the hotel lobby and get coffee while you poop if you'll do the same for me."

That's not to say people into dominance and submission, or D&S, lack a sense of fairness. Fairness has nothing to do with it, I know. It's a power exchange. Each person is getting something they want, either by assuming power or relinquishing it. My very close friend Ellen taught me all about it.

Ellen's a very pretty Colombian woman in her forties who takes her kids to hockey practice and dancing lessons like millions of other American moms. She's maybe five foot three and a hundred pounds. If you saw her on the street you might assume she sold clothes in a high-end boutique or ran a small art gallery. She's had a little fascination with dominance since she was a teenager, she told me. When she was single, she enjoyed seeing how far she could push men before they broke. For example, she'd call a guy in the middle of the night and ask him to bring her a pint of ice cream. Or she'd say she needed a ride to the airport at 6 a.m., and when the guy showed up, she would tell him the trip was canceled. Because she was very beautiful, men pretty much did what she asked them to do.

She eventually married a man who got so fed up with her "games" that he snapped and moved to Europe. Needing cash, she discovered on the Internet that she could make thousands of dollars doing what she had been doing for free. I told her I was concerned for her safety, but she assured me she wasn't working in some dungeon basement. Basically, she would go on very public dates—no sex—and treat her customers like crap.

I had made plans with her one stiflingly hot early August night in New York City. I hadn't seen her in about six months so she came in from Long Island and we decided to have a few cocktails and dinner downtown at an outdoor café. She wore a skintight black sheath and seven-inch black platform stilettos. If her hair and makeup hadn't been flawless, she would have looked like a total skank. In the middle of dinner, her phone rang and she answered it. With her hand over the microphone, she asked if I would mind if one of her clients met us for drinks. I didn't mind. I was curious to see who was on the other end of the line.

"Wear a sweater, a thick one," she said before hanging up the phone.

"Sweater?" I said. "It's gotta be ninety degrees out with no breeze and one hundred percent humidity."

"No shit, Sherlock," she said.

About a half hour later a not-at-all-bad-looking guy showed up at our table in a suit and tie—with a wool sweater under his jacket. Ellen introduced us (he said his name was John, which to this day I don't know was true or not) and he sat down. I became very uncomfortable almost immediately. I was in the middle of a business transaction with no idea what to expect or say. Was I supposed to treat him like crap too, or just Ellen? I regretted not asking her before he arrived.

Finally, I said, "Would you like a cold drink? You must be hot in that sweater."

"Thanks, I'll have a beer when the waitress comes around." He smiled a big smile full of perfectly straight bright white teeth. He reminded me of the guy who played Elaine's boyfriend in the final season of *Seinfeld*.

"How long have you known Ellen?"

"This is our," he looked at her before answering, "third?" She nodded. "Our third date."

"And what do you do for a living?" I was scared to death of letting the conversation lull out of fear that, given the opportunity, Ellen might punch him in the head or something and make a scene.

John told me he worked in banking. The waitress came by, and we ordered another round of drinks and while we drank them we talked about everything from politics to the TV shows we were watching. To any other table in the place, we probably looked like three friends catching up and sharing a few laughs, except one of us had a steady stream of perspiration running from his hairline past his ears and down his neck. The guy appeared to be crying from the top of his skull. It was actually getting painful to watch. And to make it worse, every time he would reflexively use his hand to brush a rivulet away from his eyes, Ellen would calmly stop him with a firm "No."

While we were discussing a recent episode of *The X-Files*, a drop of sweat rolled slowly down John's forehead into his left eyebrow, which at this point must have reached complete saturation because it went from his brow directly into his eye. It must have stung because he blinked his eyes really hard and pressed the knuckle of his left forefinger into his tear duct.

And as calmly as one might ask a dinner companion to pass the salt, Ellen said, "Lick my shoe."

"What?" I said.

"I wasn't talking to you." Her face was expressionless except for her lips, which had shifted slightly off-center. "Lick. My. Shoe."

John pushed his chair back from the table, noisily because the metal chair was on the concrete sidewalk. He lowered himself down on his knees and, I assume, licked Ellen's stiletto. He returned back to a seated position, still sweaty. He had a strange look on his face, like he was thinking about something that happened a long time ago.

"The bottom," Ellen said.

"Oh, God," I said, barely audibly, so that it sounded more like *Uh Guh*.

And down John went once again. Ellen smiled at me across the table as if to say, *Can you believe I get paid for this?* When he came back up to a seated position, I wanted so much to tell John to run to the bar and swish some Scotch around his mouth then haul ass to the nearest hospital and beg for a tetanus shot. But I didn't, because I was having a sort of out-of-body experience. I felt nauseated and like a third wheel, a third wheel on a boat, unnecessary and irrelevant. I paid the check and grabbed a cab as soon as I came to again.

When I stopped off at Leather Daddy's table to drop the check, he snapped it from my hand, which was the last straw.

"Look, buddy," I said, a little louder than I had intended. "You may get to treat *this guy* like a cocker spaniel, but not *me*. Got it?"

The cocker spaniel scowled at me, which really pissed me off because in my mind I was doing him a favor by helping him remember he was *on a leash. In a restaurant.* L.D. pulled a credit card out of his wallet and held it out to me without glancing up. I took it from his hand and marched to the credit card imprinter. When I filled out the slip, I put a slash through the box marked TIP/MISC. I wanted to let the guy know I didn't want his money, before he had the opportunity to stiff me.

I placed it on the table for his signature with an emotionless "Have a nice night." Neither of them responded; both were looking out the window. When they left I returned to the table with a tray to clear the remaining silverware and pick up the signed copy of the credit card slip. On a forty-five-dollar meal, they left me a twenty-dollar tip, in cash. In tiny block letters someone had written on the bill WOOF.

"What do you think that means?" I asked Robert the bartender.

"Daddy thinks you're hot," he said. "Maybe he's got an extra leash lying around, with your name on it."

"Not my type," I said.

Because I ignored the table after dropping the credit card slip, I didn't see who wrote WOOF on the twenty. I like to think Slave Boy grabbed the pen and wrote it as a message to me, but I still don't know exactly what he was trying to communicate. My best guess: *Woof, don't worry about this cocker spaniel. He's doing just fine.*

YOUR A PSYCHOPATH

A university—at least I think it was a university—recently published a study about the correlation between psychopathy and the tendency to correct other people's grammar. To be completely honest, I didn't read the study; I heard a joke about it on NPR's news quiz, *Wait Wait . . . Don't Tell Me!* And I was scrubbing a roasting pan in the kitchen sink at the time, so I might really be screwing this up. But from what I gather, the type of person who might make a snarky remark about your dangling participle is also extremely likely to have a nightstand full of human femurs.

Talk about shit you don't want to know about yourself! Correcting grammar is one of my favorite pastimes. *Damn*, I thought, *I'm a psycho and I've been completely unaware of it, all these years!* That can happen, you know. I feel like I might have seen a *Dateline* episode about it. Like, maybe I'm living a double life, hosting TV shows, writing books, walking my dog, redecorating the guest bedroom, but then without warning my brain short-circuits and I go on a killing spree. *I think an abstract floral pillow might be nice on this chaise. Boing! Must. Eat. Raw. Squirrels.* I would ask Damon if I ever come home late at night in a fugue state covered in blood, but I don't really want to know the answer.

There must be additional indicators of a psychopathic personality beyond grammar. Things that complex are never black or white. You notice that a friend writes *to* in a text message when it's obvious she meant to write *too* and before you know it you're craving fava beans and a nice Chianti? I just don't believe it! I majored in psychology for an entire semester my freshman year at Boston College, so I feel pretty qualified to determine who is and isn't a psychopath. For example, in my opinion, you're a psychopath if:

a) you correct the grammar of people you actually like or love, and

b) you do so in front of others.

Allow me to provide an example from my own life. My dad, Mike, seems to enjoy using the phrase "not for nothing." He might say during Christmas dinner something along the lines of, "Not for nothing, but I noticed your car is leaking oil. You should probably have that checked out." Do I scream, "Double negative! Double negative! Dad used a double negative!" Of course not. That would be psychotic. And also, my dad just doesn't give a crap about perfect grammar. I've noticed that if I use the word *whom* in my parents' house, he'll make an excuse to go fix something in the basement.

"You know, Dad, there's this facialist in Manhattan with whom I have the best rapport. She's a doll. The next time you and Mom come in for a visit, we should all go get facials together! It'll be a scream."

"That sounds fun, Clint. Aw, man, I just remembered that two weeks ago I smelled gas coming out of the . . . uh . . . out of the foundation. I'm gonna go check that out. Wanna help?"

"Yeah, no. I thought I'd make some crepes. Where do you keep the hazelnut flour these days?"

"You'd have to ask your mother. Terri!" (Runs down basement steps.)

The grammar I correct is mostly in my own head. If you and I strike up a conversation at a cocktail party, will I notice if your subject is singular and your verb is plural? Of course. But I won't mention it, at least not to your face. I'll just tell all my friends that, to maintain their own high social standing, they should avoid being seen with you in public. A psychopath, on the other hand, would tell you, right then and there, "In the sentence, *The bouquet of flowers he sent me are lovely*, the subject, *bouquet*, is singular and therefore takes the singular verb *is*, despite the fact that there are multiple flowers in said bouquet. The bouquet *is* lovely. See the difference?" And then he'd shove a shiv in your liver while reaching for another canapé.

I'm glad we talked this out because I'm feeling much better about myself. Whew, I'm not a psycho! Yay! There is an exception, though, to my self-imposed not-in-public rule: complete strangers who have decided to tell me via social media just how much I suck at life.

Because I make my living on TV, certain members of the population find it socially acceptable to spew vitriol in my general direction online. And before I go any further, I must say that 99.99 percent of all the comments I receive on social media are either positive or extremely positive, which is amazing. The only public figures with higher favorability percentages than mine are Betty White and that little kid who got high on nitrous oxide at the dentist's office. So, I'm truly grateful that the vast majority of people who choose to communicate with me are respectful and polite, but as Mike would say, not for nothing, that teeny sliver of a minority can be really fucking annoying.

And no, my feelings aren't easily hurt or anything. (Spend thirteen years in the television industry, and you too can develop the thick layer of emotional callouses necessary for a successful career!) If you don't like my sense of humor, I don't care. If you don't like my clothes, I don't care. If you don't like my sexuality, I don't care. If it makes you feel better about yourself to tell me I'm a worthless sack of crap, knock yourself out. But I'd prefer you do it using your real name, with your actual photo, and in impeccable English. Which never happens.

For example, I received this message on Facebook from a woman named Irene with two friends and a cat avatar:

> Your always talking about drinking on the chew. I hope you get fired because your a alkahalic and a idiot.

To which I replied:

> Dear Madam,
>
> Thank you for your lovely note. Please allow me to address your two main points forthwith.
>
> The National Institute on Alcohol Abuse and Alcoholism suggests that men not exceed four drinks per day or a total of fourteen per week. Most weeks I consume less than half that amount. Nevertheless, I appreciate your implied concern.
>
> If your hopes and dreams include me being fired from my job, I encourage you to share them with the executives at ABC/Disney. For best results, you may want to include in your correspondence reasons for my termination other than your belief that I am "a idiot."
>
> Because you have been so kind as to share your opinion of me directly with me, cutting out any middleman, I hope you will allow me to return the favor. Granted, I

know less about you than you may about me, but what little I do know is rather telling. Mostly, I am aware that the public education system in your state has failed you miserably, and for that I am sorry, not just for you, but for our country as a whole. Because you seem to have been denied English class after the fifth grade, I am happy to provide you with some of the highlights:

Your is a possessive pronoun. That is, it indicates that someone or something belongs to you. For example, one might refer to *your* cat figurine collection, *your* bedsores, or *your* belief that Tom Selleck can hear your heart's lustful cries for him.

You're is a contraction of the words *you* and *are*. For example, instead of writing *You are apparently unaware of any software that might correct blatant spelling errors.* To adopt a more conversational tone, I can write, *You're apparently unaware . . .* You get the idea, I hope.

Proper nouns, such as the titles of TV shows, are always capitalized. Words beginning with a vowel receive the article *an.* And there is no *k* in the words *alcohol or alcoholic.* There is, however, a *k* in Alka-Seltzer. Speaking of which, I need some. Wow, do I have the mother of hangovers today! Remind me never to mix tequila, bath salts, and Venezuelan hookers ever again.

Until our electronic paths cross again, I wish you peace.

Sincerely,

Clinton

SALAD DAYS

For a couple of years, I was a spokesman for a brand of pre-packaged salads—combinations of the more popular lettuces, sometimes including a smattering of shredded carrots, all conveniently washed and cellophane-wrapped for the health-conscious man or woman on the go! The gig paid pretty well, and I liked the work: developing salad recipes, posing for a few photos while holding salad, and being interviewed by journalists about, yes, salad. Easy, if typical, spokesman stuff. To mix things up a bit, I tried to convince the salad marketing team to think outside the plastic bag and sponsor a contest I could host called the Great American Toss Off, during which hundreds, maybe thousands, of really gorgeous people could slather themselves in ranch dressing and frolic in a giant swimming pool filled with arugula. I would watch that *all damn day*, I said, but they didn't bite.

Instead, the company held a more straightforward contest: Tell us why YOU love salad and you could win a trip for two to Napa Valley! While there, the winners would go wine tasting, take a cooking course at the Culinary Institute of America, and receive a styling lesson from me.

About a week before I was supposed to fly out to California, I called my endorsements agent at the time, Jason, to confirm some of the details of the trip, specifically the expectations surrounding this "styling lesson." I had assumed it was the "How to Dress Your Body Type" speech I had given dozens of times across the country.

"Not quite," Jason said. "They want you to talk about styling your salad."

"I don't know what that means," I answered.

"You know, how to make your salad look pretty."

It took me slightly longer than usual to process the words that had just come out of his mouth. "That's ridiculous. How long am I supposed to talk about this?"

"You're contracted for two hours."

There are things I can drone on about *ad nauseam*, but decorating lettuce is not one of them. "Two hours? You have got to be kidding me," I said. "You make salad *look pretty* by putting it on a nice plate and sprinkling some . . . I don't know . . . chopped pecans on top. Now, how long did it take me to say that? Three seconds, max? What am I going to do for the other one hour, fifty-nine minutes, and fifty-seven seconds?"

Eventually Jason calmed me down, by basically lying through his teeth. "They'll be so glad you're there," he said. "You can talk about whatever you want, salad, clothes, decorating. Just talk and smile. Get your picture taken. Then cash the check."

I'll be honest; that part about the check made me feel a lot better about the whole situation.

When I arrived at the culinary institute on the Sunday morning of the grand-prize weekend, the contest winners and their guests were watching a chef cook a pork loin. So I took the opportunity to ask the organizer to clarify my role. After the demo, she said, the winners were going to create their own salads, using the prepackaged blends (of course), and I would help them with their plating, because each salad would be professionally photographed.

"Do you have a nice selection of plates?" I asked. I had told my agent the marketing team should supply me with as many options as possible. Plates, theoretically, could go a long way in salad styling. "Maybe some pretty colors? I could show them how to mix and match patterns. Or create an interesting table with a combination of antique and modern pieces."

"All the plates are white," she said.

I took a deep breath through my nose, while nodding and smiling in hopes of disguising my blinding rage. "Okay. That's cool," I said. "I'm just curious if Jason had mentioned having a big selection to pull from."

"He did," the organizer said, "but we decided that the plates should be white to really showcase the salads themselves. And we don't want you to do the salad styling for the winners, we want you to *inspire* people to use the plate that best reflects their vision."

So, for two hours, I walked around an industrial kitchen, interrupting couples who were grilling shrimp or searing steaks or whisking vinaigrettes to suggest different white plates.

"You know what would look *amazing* under that salad," I said to a mother and daughter. "This plate because . . . it's a *triangle*. And how often do you see *that*? Not often enough, if you ask me. Think about the significance. Earth, wind, fire. Father, Son, Holy Spirit. It can symbolize whatever you want."

After an hour or so, I tried fanning the flames of not-so-friendly competition among the breeders. "See that couple over there?" I asked a late-thirties husband and wife from Michigan, whispering and nodding my head toward a couple of newlyweds from Florida. "They're using a high-gloss oversized round. Big mistake. *Huge.* Who's going to be looking at their salad when it's on top of that gaudy thing? Ah, but *this* plate. It's *ivory* with a matte finish and not too much rim. There's no way *this* plate is going to steal *your* salad's thunder."

They looked at me as one might have expected them to, like I was batshit.

Two hours felt like a thousand days and nights. Basically, I was the Scheherazade of Salad, just making up nonsense to avoid not death, but a breach of contract lawsuit. I needed a drink, a massage, a pill. Pretty much anything to make this day go away. Luckily, my friend Lisa was awaiting my return in the very expensive hotel room where we were staying. Usually if there's a companion airline ticket included in an appearance deal, and I'm traveling somewhere fun or beautiful, Damon will come with me. But he had recently entered the final stretch of writing his dissertation, so he asked if I would mind terribly if he sat this trip out. I didn't mind at all. I was thrilled he was *this close* to finishing his doctoral degree. It was hard to believe, but after eight years of his studying and researching, I might someday live in a home without twenty oversized textbooks and huge piles of psychology journals cluttering the dining room table. "Do what you need to do," I told him, mimicking Ingrid Bergman's *Casablanca* stare. "I'll miss you, darling."

Lisa was thrilled to accompany me in Damon's stead. She always is. Doesn't matter where we're headed. I once brought her with me to a mall in Milwaukee, and you would have thought she was strolling the Champs Élysées. "I'm just glad to get away from the trolls for a few days," she said when I asked why she was skipping through the mall. "The little sons of bitches always want so much from me, like food and . . . well, food." The trolls were her two teenage sons. She'd left them fifty bucks and her car keys on the kitchen counter with a note that said, "Good luck, fuckers. I'm out."

While I'd been degrading myself in the promotion of leafy greens, Lisa had been renting movies in our hotel suite and ordering room service. "I just watched an entire Japanese film—in Japanese. No subtitles. While eating a Kobe beef burger," she said when I got back to the room. "This may just be the best day of my life."

I kicked off my shoes and picked at the cold fries on her plate.

"How was your day, America's Sweetheart?"

"Stupid," I said.

"Well, let's go do something. We could sit by the pool. Or get drunk. Or both."

All were perfectly agreeable suggestions, but I had been hoping to have a mud bath in a spa I liked a few miles up the road in Calistoga. I called to check their availability, and they were booked for the day. So I called two other spas. Still no luck. At the fourth spa, they had one appointment open, but there was a catch. I consulted with Lisa.

"They only have one appointment," I said, holding my hand over the microphone. "And it's for couples."

"What's the problem," she said. "We're a couple. A couple of *assholes*."

I booked the mud baths, unsure why I even hesitated in the first place. Having been best friends continuously since junior high, Lisa and I are like two peas in a twisted pod. We often tell people, hospitality workers mostly, that we're married, just to watch the expression on their faces slowly change from coolly welcoming to wholly confused. "We're on our honeymoon," she proudly stated to a maître d' in Honolulu, while I stood behind her braiding a little strand of her hair. "We're celebrating our twenty-fifth," I once confided to a concierge in Key West, "but, please, don't tell anyone. We're keeping it hush-hush for obvious reasons." He answered, "Twenty-fifth *what*?" In reply, I stuck my tongue in my cheek and wriggled it around a bit. It just seemed like the right thing to do. He didn't ask any follow-ups.

The girl behind the front desk of the spa was pretty and young. She struck me as the type who played varsity field hockey: long, lean, no makeup, and a golden tan. Her name tag said BRITANEY and so I immediately hated her parents.

"Oh. My. God. You're from *What Not to Wear*," she said when we checked in.

"That's me."

"Oh. My. God. I love that show. I always wanted to nominate my mother. She needs you, like, so bad. She wears sweatshirts and mom jeans. All. The. Time."

Because approximately five thousand teenage girls tell me that every year, I have a pat answer: "You should totally go to our website. There's, like, a form for that. And I shit you not: We actually read every nomination."

"I'm so doing that," Britaney said. I knew she wouldn't. That's why I didn't feel bad about lying to her. The producers would never even consider flying twenty crew members in from New York to ambush some dumpy mom in Calistoga. If she had lived closer to a major airport, maybe. And only if the casting department could find three other women nearby with different style problems. What I wanted to say more than anything else was, *Don't worry about your mother, Britaney. Save yourself. Save your goddamn self!*

"You're signed up for a couple's mud bath," she said after checking her ledger.

"Yup."

"It's for two," she said, by way of clarification, I suppose.

"I'm one," I said. "And she's two."

Lisa chimed in: "And we can't *wait* to get naked together. Do we take off our clothes here? Because I can."

"No," said Britaney. "Please don't. I'll show you to your room."

She led us down a long hall to a private vestibule for getting undressed that connected via a wooden door to the treatment room itself. Inside it were a large L-shaped mud bath, a curtain-less shower, and a bubbling mineral tub big enough for two, which were to be used in that order. Mud, rinse, soak. "If you need anything, just call," Britaney said, without pointing to a phone or intercom of any sort.

Despite what we tell certain service professionals, Lisa and I aren't exactly *comfortable* being naked around each other. Sure, we had gone skinny-dipping in the ocean together for years— we spent practically every warm day together at Smith's Point Beach on the south shore of Long Island throughout high school and when I was home from college—but our swimwear never came off until after we were submerged up to our chins in the water. Then, we'd float for hours, holding our bathing suits in our hands and laughing about the horny electric eels and pecker-craving piranha lurking, unseen, beneath the surface.

We undressed quickly, facing opposite directions, and I grabbed a white waffle-knit robe from the peg near the door. "See you inside," I said and sprinted into the treatment room.

A combination of volcanic ash and earthy peat, the mud was dense and dark but also rather fluffy—and hot, thanks to the scalding, mineral-rich water that was pumped in from an underground geothermal spring. Once properly submerged, I had the sensation of being trapped inside a soaking wet, sulfur-stinking sponge, which is more enjoyable than it sounds if you're willing to believe the environmental and psychological toxins you've been hoarding are fleeing your body like bats out of a smoky cave. *Make me feel better about my life, mud gods. I don't want to be a salad whore anymore.*

Lisa entered after I had placed two cucumber slices and a cool, damp washcloth over my eyes. "Now what?" she said.

"You do the Dance of the Seven Veils. What do you think, you do? Get in."

"How do I do that, smart ass? This thing's taller than I am." The tub had a wide flat edge, covered in white tile, which rose about three feet above the ground. At six foot four, I was able to step right over it. For Lisa, five feet tall on a good day, it wouldn't be so easy.

"Hop up on the side, swing your legs in, then lie down like I am."

From the sound of it, grunting mostly, Lisa was taking my advice. "OK, I'm in," she said, "but this doesn't seem right. I'm just sort of lying on top."

I laughed. I neglected to mention that you don't really sink into the mud. "You've got to wriggle your butt down into it. Really jam it in there."

"This is ridiculous." After an extended period of moaning and breathing heavily, she said, "This motherfuckin' mud is hot as *hell*. Why didn't you tell me it would be this hot?"

"Why don't you just shut up and relax. You're ruining my spa experience."

"Oh, I will ruin your spa experience, all right. And when they do the autopsy on your body, they're gonna find mud in places you never knew existed."

Usually, I enjoy Lisa's empty threats, but she was starting to get on my nerves. I wasn't even close to becoming detoxified.

"No, really. Are you ever going to stop talking? Or is that trap of yours set to run for the full forty-five minutes?"

"Oh, I still have more to say, dick whistle. This stuff *reeks*. You just spent three hundred bucks so we could steep ourselves in a giant pile of steaming horseshit."

I let out a groan and stopped responding. Eventually Lisa went silent. She was either dead or exhausted, and I was grateful either way. We lay in our tub at a right angle, our toes pointed toward each other, for about twenty minutes. Once sufficiently overheated and pleasantly light-headed, I removed the washcloth and cucumbers from my eyes and checked to make sure Lisa's were still covered. I stood up and with my hands and forearms wiped from my naked body the excess mud, which fell back into the tub in thick glops. I jauntily stepped over to the shower, my back to Lisa, and rinsed the remaining mud from my newly detoxed cracks and crevices.

"I'm getting into the Jacuzzi now," I announced.

"Good for you, princess," she said. "I'm getting out of here before a redwood takes root in my vagina."

"OK, I'll shut my eyes."

The first sound I heard from Lisa's direction was barely audible over the motor of the mineral bath. It was the kind of noise a middle-aged man might make getting out of bed after a solid sleep. *Uuuunnnngh.* The second sounded more like the first guttural emanations of a German charwoman suffering an appendicitis attack. *Aaaaaooo guhhhhpffft.* And the third, the final audible cry of an elderly bison as it submits to a pack of hungry coyote. *Mmmmbuh.*

"Are you OK over there?" I asked.

"Pawk," she said. "I'm stuck."

* * *

Lisa and I have been calling each other Pawk for more than twenty years now. I am Pawk. She is Pawk. And together we are Pawk. It's pronounced the way people with thick New York accents say *pork*.

The name stuck after a visit to our friend Sandra's condo on Long Island. She had just given birth to her second son, Vincent, affectionately referred to as Baby Bincent by Isabel's first son, Nicholas.

As soon as we sat down on the living room sofa, Nicholas, who was almost three and excited to receive company, brought Lisa and me one of his toys, a colorful limp-limbed clown.

"That's one of his favorites," Sandra said tepidly. She was nursing Vincent in a nearby chair. Her normally well-maintained hair was stringy and she looked like she was having trouble staying awake. "It speaks if you squeeze it." Sandra, still in her early twenties, was the first of our high school cohort to have children, so her situation was foreign and awkward to us.

Evidently, the purpose of the doll was to teach some basic anatomy. When you squeezed its hand, you activated some microchip and the doll said, "Hand!" If you squeezed its leg, the doll said, "Leg!" Lisa and I must have been thinking the same thing, because she whispered in my ear: "Do you think this thing is anatomically correct?"

I replied, "Did you squeeze its . . . you know?"

"That's the *first* place I squeezed. It's dead down there."

Playing with Nicholas, we could ignore the fact Sandra was married, with two small humans to keep alive. Responsibility frightened us. So, we kept squeezing.

"Head!" said the doll.

"Head!" yelled Nicholas.

"Head!" cheered Lisa and I.

Squeeze.

"Hand!" said the doll.

"Hand!" yelled Nicholas.

"Hand!" cheered Lisa and I.

Squeeze.

"Tummy!" said the doll.

"Tummy!" yelled Nicholas.

"Tummy!" cheered Lisa and I.

Nicholas was getting all riled up, twirling around the living room with his hands in the air. His joy was contagious because we were all laughing like a bunch of kids on a playground. Then Lisa pressed the doll's shoe.

"Foot! Foot!" said the doll. Apparently it had a glitch in that extremity because it said foot twice. Or maybe it was just ticklish.

Nicholas stopped in his tracks and stared at both of us.

"Pawk," he announced, the way one might answer the question of what's for dinner.

"What did he just say?" I asked Sandra. She shrugged.

"Pawk!" Nicholas yelled.

Lisa and I looked at each other. Then back at Nicholas. Then back at each other.

"Pawk!" we cried in unison.

We've been Pawk ever since.

"Pawk, I'm stuck."

"You're not stuck," I assured her. "Just try harder."

"I'm trying as hard as I can. I'm dying. In the mud."

"Would you like me to call an ambulance?"

"Funny, douche canoe. But I'm not kidding. Help me out of here!"

"OK, OK," I said, more than mildly annoyed. "Close your eyes!" I climbed out of the Jacuzzi and reached for my robe, which I had hung on a nearby hook. It looked so clean and white and soft. If I wore it to pull Pawk from the mud, it would get filthy. *That's not the way this should go*, I thought. *I want a pristine robe after my mineral bath.* And so I decided to remain naked.

"Keep your eyes closed. I'm coming over," I said.

"I honestly have no desire to see your dick. Just get me out of here before I fucking boil."

During all of her grunting and groaning, Lisa had managed to swing her legs over the side of the tub. She must have inverted her center of gravity because her head was thrown back into the mud, her frizzy copper hair splayed around her like a slow-burning fire. As I gazed down upon her she struck me as a giant overturned turtle slowly sinking into a prehistoric tar pit.

"Oh, that's not good," I said. I couldn't help but laugh. "Give me your hands and I'll pull you up." She raised her arms from her sides. I took hold of her wrists and she took mine. I steadied myself as best I could on the slick concrete floor and pulled. Her shoulders barely broke the surface. "You're gonna have to help me out a bit here," I told her.

"I'm trying," she growled. And opened her eyes.

"You're peeking!" I yelled.

"I can't see anything except the ceiling!"

"Well, shut your eyes anyway."

"Why do you get to have *your* eyes open?"

"How am I supposed to pull you out without looking?"

"Oh, I don't even care at this point."

"Believe me, it's not like I *want* to see any of this."

Now's probably a good time for me to add that Lisa is not a small girl. And I'm not saying this with any judgment, because life happens and I adore her. But whenever I picture her in my head, I see her as she was when we were young, a little wisp of a thing, five feet tall and ninety pounds soaking wet. After thirty years, two kids, a bad marriage, and a decade of working over-nights in a hospital, she's put on some weight, much of it in the bust region. Lisa doesn't say whether she minds it or not, though she will frequently note that many men are drawn to it. I, on the other hand, was doing everything in my power to avoid looking at it.

I propped my foot up on the tub, between where Lisa's legs were dangling over the edge, and pulled as hard as I could.

"Puuuuuush!" I yelled.

"You're hurting meeee!" she yelled.

I kept pulling and she kept falling back into the mud, again and again, until we were both laughing so hard we had to pause, twice, to catch our breath.

"I don't know how much longer I can keep this up," I said after ten minutes.

"Let's give it one more try. Really put your back into it this time."

"You need to squeeze your abs more."

"Oh, shut up."

Like one of those mothers who summons enough adrena-line to lift a Volkswagen off her kid's leg, I found the strength to pull Pawk from her bog. One might think I deserved a heartfelt thank-you from my oldest friend in the world. Instead, Lisa—covered in so much mud that only the whites of her eyes resem-bled human tissue—asked: "Do your balls *always* hang that low?"

"It's *hot* in here," I said, covering my junk.

"Because, wow. That's . . . really something."

"It's not too late for me to drown you," I said.

Back in the reception area, Britaney told us we looked refreshed. We thanked her and said we enjoyed ourselves. I was halfway out the door, when I stuck my head back in. "Don't forget to nominate your mother for the show," I said.

"I won't!" she answered.

Pawk went back to our hotel, where we split a bottle of wine and fell asleep before sunset, our salad days far behind us.

RICH AND FAMOUS

A few years ago the principal of the high school I attended asked my sister Courtney, whom he knew through a friend of a friend, to ask me to deliver the commencement address. Whether intentional or not, taking this route was a smart move on his part. Courtney could basically ask for both my kidneys and I'd carve them out myself. Oh, you want to use them as bookends? In the guest bedroom? That's cool. Would you also like my pancreas? It might make a good doorstop. No? OK. Just let me know if you change your mind.

But even coming from Courtney, this request seemed like a huge imposition. You see, I loathe teenagers. Can't stand the sight of them. If you don't count rapists, murderers, KKK members, terrorists, child molesters, religious extremists, animal abusers, most celebrity chefs, all Kardashians, bankers, career politicians, and people who market sugary breakfast foods to children, teenagers are hands down the worst humans on the planet. Being in the general vicinity of just one pimply-faced bag of hormones is enough to provoke stirrings of diarrhea in my lower intestine. Four hundred at once?

"No fucking way," I told Courtney.

"What? Why not?" she asked, sounding more surprised than I would have expected.

"Because. I don't want to go back there."

"This again," she said. I could feel her rolling her eyes on the other end of the telephone. "They're not asking you to travel back in time and repeat puberty, just give an inspirational speech. 'I'm Clinton Kelly. Congratulations. The best years of your life are ahead of you. Blah, blah, bullshit, bullshit, bye.'"

"I don't want to." Wow, that sounded whiney even to me.

"Oh, my God," she said with a laugh. "You're being such a . . . dork."

Perhaps, but that's familiar territory.

When Courtney was born, I was thirteen and having a rough time in junior high. By the eighth grade I had neither mastered the social game of adolescence (destroy others lest you be destroyed) nor fully constructed the persona that would eventually allow me to cope with the horrors of high school (that I was a member of the upper-middle class who had somehow found himself, through no fault of his own, living in a squarely middle-class town). Mostly, I was horrified by the way kids my age behaved toward one another. Pushing, shoving, cursing, name-calling. It was all so vulgar. Once, a guy named Steve—in home economics, of all classes—whispered in my ear that he was going to rape my mother. I asked for a bathroom pass and cried in the boys' room until the period ended, not because I thought he would actually do it, but because the kind of person who would say such a thing actually existed in the world.

The way I saw it, Courtney was an innocent soul entrusted

into my care, at least when my parents left us home alone to meet friends for dinner. I was determined to construct for my baby sister a future free of humiliation and sadness.

When she was three, I would sit with Courtney for hours flipping through magazines and catalogs playing a game I had invented for her called Pick One. At every spread, she had to choose from the two pages the one she liked better. This task would make her confident and decisive, I told myself. Some choices were easy, like a page of dense women's-magazine text opposite an advertisement for tampons. "This one," she'd say, pointing to the tampon ad, because in it a woman smiled ear to ear while riding a bicycle. Tampons are fun! But some decisions were more difficult, like when it came to the Toys"R"Us catalog. On the left, an Easy-Bake Oven; on the right, a Barbie Townhouse.

"You can only pick one page," I'd say. "You have to make your decision and live with it forever." The pressure was for her own good.

"The Barbie house." She looked up at me for signs of approval. I gave her a slight smile as if to say, *Whatever you choose is the right choice.* But in my heart, I was doing backflips in piles of glitter. *Yes! The townhouse! An oven without a house attached? How stupid. And that stove is so old-fashioned. A townhouse would have a modern oven in it, something with a convection setting, plus lots more fun stuff, like a private elevator! And if you played your cards right—kept yourself thin, learned how to toss your hair at cocktail parties—you could probably marry a rich man and hire a servant to do all the cooking for you.*

Another favorite game of ours was called Would You Rather, in which one of us would present two death-related scenarios and the other would choose the preferable demise. For example,

I might ask my four-year-old sister: "Would you rather die being pecked to death by crows or drowning in a kiddie pool full of puke and orange soda?"

"Orange soda," she'd answer. "Would you rather get shot in the head or stabbed in the heart?"

"In the head," I'd say, "any day of the week."

Courtney and I also spent a lot of time practicing cheer-leading moves in the backyard. "When you jump, keep your elbows bent," I'd tell her. "I'll lift you up from there and then you can stand on my shoulders. Got it?" She would nod, her big green eyes unblinking. She looked like one of those paintings in our pediatrician's office. "And what do you yell when you're up there?"

"Go, defense!"

"Right!" I had never watched a football game in my life, nor did I intend to. I knew approximately four football-related words. Defense, tackle, touchdown, and . . . ummm . . . ball. So we just rotated through those, Courtney shouting from atop my shoulders: "Get the ball! Yay, a touchdown! Tackle that bastard!" I was going to make sure Courtney became a cheerleader if I had to become a hunchback in the process—because cheerleaders, I was certain at the time, didn't have a worry in the world.

Occasionally Terri would open the back door to check on us, the corded kitchen phone wedged against her ear. She was going through a phase in which she had to spend every waking moment talking to her friend—and our former housemate—Lynn. Though Terri and Lynn had each remarried, they seemed to be having a difficult time living five miles apart. No subject, however mundane or highly personal, was off-limits between those two, which was most likely the reason my sister Jodi barely left her room between the ages of twelve and sixteen. They were obsessed with their daughters' pubescent developments. On any given day in our kitchen you might hear one side of the conversation that went something like this: "I'm making chicken cutlets for dinner. What are you making? . . . Pork is nice, as long as you don't overcook it. . . . Bra shopping? How did that go? . . . Oh, Candice is a C? Jodi's still a B-cup, but I'm sure she'll be a full C by the time she finishes high school. That's what I was. You know, any bigger and a different kind of man is interested . . ."

And on it went, all day. The backyard was my and Courtney's only escape from talk of suburban homemaking and fourteen-year-old-girl parts.

"Could you please not kill your sister," Terri would call out to me.

"I'll try, Mom," I'd yell back.

"I don't know what he's doing. He's got her hair in pigtails and he's throwing her around the yard." She shut the door.

By the time I left for college, I felt pretty sure I had aimed Courtney directly toward my—I mean, her—target: unparalleled popularity! How could she not hit the mark? She exuded all the qualities I never possessed in high school: Self-confidence! Joie de vivre! Willpower! A steely poker face when confronted with disappointed authority figures! (If my parents told me they were "disappointed" in me, I would immediately burst into grotesque sobs. But not Courtney. She would look you straight in the eyes like, *You think I give a crap about your opinion of me?*) Granted, she was only six, but the kid had star quality.

I don't know too much about Courtney's high school years because I was in my late twenties by that time, and wholly obsessed with my own love life, career, body, social life, and future. Jodi had moved to Japan after college, and I was living in New York City, so Courtney was basically raised by my parents as an only child. She and I would talk on a regular basis, however, so I knew she was a captain of the cheerleading squad and quite popular. And while she could be sweet and silly around me, I could recognize in her when she spoke about the social dynamics of high school a certain ruthlessness, and a weariness, as if staying on top of the pile was taking its toll. I was so proud of her and yet I felt profoundly sorry for her. I guess I had forgotten to mention, after moving out and moving past, that I was just kidding. Those games we had played, they were just games.

Life went on, as it tends to, if you're lucky. Courtney married her high school boyfriend after she graduated from college. Today they have two beautiful sons, the older one named Clinton. I got a little choked up when they announced that decision. We talk all the time about things like our marriages and her kids and our parents and our mutual love of wallpaper. And once in a while she asks her big brother for a favor.

"I don't know, Courtney. High school was different for me," I said. "You don't understand."

She was quiet on the other end of the line, then said, "You're right. I probably don't completely understand, but I think it would be a nice thing for you to do. There are probably a bunch of kids in this class who hate high school as much as you did. Do it for them. Besides, you're rich and famous. Who the hell cares what a few brats think of you?"

I accepted the invitation and regretted it immediately. So, I stopped thinking about it until the morning of the graduation ceremony, when I couldn't ignore it any longer. What did I want to say? What did these kids want to hear? What were they capable of hearing? Would anyone heckle me? Could I cancel? Would they understand just how chic a mustard-brown cap-toe oxford is, especially when paired with a light-gray checked suit?

"Thank you so much for inviting me here today," I began. "It really is an honor and a pleasure to speak to the Comsewogue Class of 2014 as you embark upon the next phase of your journey into adulthood. I graduated from this very school in 1987. Every guy had a mullet. Every girl had a perm. And the school looked exactly as it does today, like a Lithuanian prison.

"Because I graduated twenty-seven years ago, I'm roughly the same age as your parents, which quite frankly is very . . . how do I say this . . . depressing. Like really, really depressing. Have you seen those people? They are so *old*. But I won't be too rough on them because I suppose they're good people. I don't know that for sure, but you're here and not in jail so they can't be all that bad.

"As I was thinking about what to say to you today, I realized that when I was your age, I never would have taken the advice of some dude who was forty-five. Gross. But I would have listened to that old guy if he told me how to become rich and famous. So, Comsewogue Class of 2014, today I am going to share with you the secrets of becoming rich and famous!

"Secret Number One: Dump the Fucking Assholes.

"Dump 'em! There are people in your life who make you feel great about yourself. Keep them around. For as long as possible. Then there are people who will drain your life force, drop by drop, because making you feel empty makes them feel full. Life is a little screwed up like that. But you have a choice today, and every day until your last day on earth, when you find yourself in the company of someone who makes you feel fat or stupid or ugly or worthless or untalented to say, perhaps not even aloud, 'You're a real fucking asshole, and I want absolutely nothing to do with you. Have a nice life, because I'm outta here, douchebag.'

"And if you happen to be dating an asshole, dump him or dump her tonight. And whatever you do, don't make babies with an asshole. You will be stuck with the asshole for eighteen years, at least.

"Secret Number Two of Becoming Rich and Famous: Don't Be a Fucking Asshole.

"Everybody here today—every student, parent, teacher, grandparent, television host—is guilty of being an asshole at one point or another. We all say insensitive things every once in a while. We all commit little acts that hurt each other from time to time. But your mission, if you choose to accept it, is to be an asshole as rarely as possible.

"First of all, it's just the right thing to do, but that might not be enough to convince you. So I will tell you what your parents might not have told you: Not being an asshole can make you more money. When people like you, they give you jobs, they give you raises, they give you promotions, they buy your products.

"And that's not all! Not being an asshole will make you hotter. I'm not kidding. I went to my twenty-year high school reunion, and all the nicest people were exponentially better-looking than the people who were assholes. It was actually kind of shocking. So if you don't want to be nice because it's the right thing to do, be nice because the alternative is that you end up all busted twenty years from now.

"Secret Number Three of Becoming Rich and Famous: Forget Everything Bad That Has Ever Happened to You.

"If that sounds impossible to do, you are right. But aspire to it anyway. When you wake up tomorrow morning, you can spend your energy thinking about all the people who have done you wrong: the teacher who gave you a C when you deserved an A; the popular kid who called you a dork; or worse, the coach that never understood your value to the team. You can think about all that stuff—but you will never be able to change it.

"The energy you spend with your head in the past will never get you closer to the future you dream for yourself. I have been called every name in the book, and I honestly don't care because . . . What you think of me says more about you than it does about me.

"I'll repeat that. What you think about me says more about you than it does about me.

"That thought might be too deep for you right now, but someday it's gonna click and you're gonna be like, *That Clinton Kelly is a fucking genius!* And I'm gonna be like, *Yeah, no shit.*

"Secret Number Four of Becoming Rich and Famous: Do What You Love.

"It's as simple as that. If you are going off to college this fall to study accounting because you love numbers and spreadsheets and tax law, that is awesome. If you are going off to college this fall to study accounting because your parents convinced you it will lead to a steady job with good benefits and a 401(k) plan, you . . . are . . . screwed.

"You'll probably have to work forty-five years, at least, until you retire. That's a long time to do something you hate. Find something that makes you happy, whether it's writing or cars or flowers or sports or fashion or science or travel and do something related to that. Trust me, life is so much more fun when you're doing something you love.

"Now, I have a confession to make. I've been lying to you. Those are not the secrets to becoming rich and famous. They are the secrets to becoming ridiculously happy, which is so much more important. And let's be honest, you wouldn't have listened to me if I had started this speech by saying, 'These are the four secrets to happiness.' Lame.

"And I guess that's all. Have a nice life, dipshits!"

The afternoon was sunny and warm, so graduation was held outside on the football field. As I walked across the lawn to the folding chair with my name on it, I couldn't help but quietly laugh at the absurdity of it all. Me on a football field in a two-thousand-dollar suit. Boys in blue caps and gowns, girls in gold. The marching band playing "Pomp and Circumstance." Parents, grandparents, siblings sitting on bleachers. My parents and Courtney were out there, too, somewhere, but I couldn't pick them out of the crowd. It was all so solemn, this rite of passage, as if these four hundred kids were being sent off to fight some epic battle, which of course they were. A battle to be the kind of human you want to be, to fight the fights worth fighting. Maybe a few of them were aware of that, but I doubted it. What did I know at their age? Not much more than that I wanted out, never to return.

Yet here I was. Back and bigger than ever. And why did I hate it so much in the first place again? It was getting harder and harder to remember. Because kids are jerks? Maybe. But, I've learned, as we all must, that adults are jerks too. At least some of them. And that's why I feel so strongly that if you have the opportunity to surround yourself with people who aren't jerks, you should not just take it, but grab it, seize it, squeeze the living hell out of it.

I met my parents and Courtney at a local restaurant. They had made an early reservation because Courtney's husband was watching their kids. When the waitress delivered our drinks,

Mike raised his and said, "Excellent speech, son. I'm very proud of you."

"Thanks, Dad," I said.

"You should take that speech on the road. There's big money in graduation speeches. Did they pay you for that?"

"No, Dad. I did it for free."

He shrugged. "Next time."

"That's a beautiful suit," Terri said. "They're making pant legs narrow again. I like that. It looked very expensive even from far away."

"Thanks, Mom," I said. I really was glad to hear it. "What about you, Courtney? What did you think of my speech?"

She smiled a sly smile. "If you gave that speech at my graduation," she said, "I would have thought you were pretty cool."

"Really?" I asked.

"Yeah, really."

"Did you hear that, Mom and Dad? The captain of the cheerleaders thinks I'm coooooool."

Everyone laughed. "You're such a spaz," Courtney said. "Let's order dinner. I want to be home in time to kiss the boys good night." So we all opened our menus. There seemed to be a few dozen more options than necessary. Courtney closed hers within fifteen seconds.

"That was quick," I said. "Do you know what you want already?"

"Yep. I'm having the salmon."

"That's such a grown-up choice," I said.

She looked at me and scrunched up her nose. "You do realize I'm thirty-three, don't you?"

"Of course." Thirty-three. Eighteen. Six. What's the difference, really.

AFTERWORD

Dear Grandma,

I'm sorry for all the foul language. I hope you don't think less of me after reading this.

Love,

Clinton

PS: I didn't tell any of our stories because I can't bear to share them with anyone. You're all mine.

ACKNOWLEDGMENTS

Thank you so freakin' much:

Kate Dresser, my editor at Gallery Books, for the sage advice regarding the structure and tone of several of these essays. And for your limitless patience with my missed deadlines. And for letting me include some fiction. And for not taking it personally when I completely avoided your phone calls and e-mails for, like, six months. Sorry. I can be ostrich-y at times.

Jen Bergstrom, at Gallery, for asking me to write this book in the first place. Most of all, however, I will always be most thankful for you inspiring me to adopt a dog all those years ago. "If Jen Bergstrom can do it," I told Damon, "we *certainly* can!" (I meant it as a compliment.)

Jen Robinson, at Gallery, for being a superstar publicist. I always enjoy our car rides together when you can give me the dirt on other authors, like when [REDACTED] and you were on tour and she [REDACTED] with [REDACTED].

Lauren Galit, my longtime literary agent and longer-time friend, for always being such a calming influence on me. You're a fantastic cheerleader because you're not manic or a bitch.

Bob Chibka, my former professor at BC and current friend, for making me want to be a better writer.

Infinite thanks to Mike and Terri for all the laughs over the years, but mostly for being the most supportive and encouraging parents a guy could ever ask for.

My sisters, Jodi and Courtney, I want you to know how incredibly proud of the intelligent, strong, kind women you've become. I'd do anything for you and your beautiful families.

Damon, the smartest decision I ever made was hitching my rickety old wagon to your brilliant star. I love you. Beyond.